Contagious Selling

HOW TO TURN A CONNECTION INTO A RELATIONSHIP THAT LASTS A LIFETIME

DAVID A. RICH

Mc
Graw
Hill

New York   Chicago   San Francisco   Lisbon   London   Madrid   Mexico City
Milan   New Delhi   San Juan   Seoul   Singapore   Sydney   Toronto

Copyright © 2013 by the McGraw-Hill Companies, Inc. All rights reserved. Printed in the United States of America. Except as permitted under the United States Copyright Act of 1976, no part of this publication may be reproduced or distributed in any form or by any means, or stored in a database or retrieval system, without the prior written permission of the publisher.

1 2 3 4 5 6 7 8 9 0   DOC/DOC   1 0 9 8 7 6 5 4 3 2

ISBN: 978-0-07-179695-8
MHID: 0-07-179695-9

e-ISBN: 978-0-07-179696-5
e-MHID: 0-07-179696-7

McGraw-Hill books are available at special quantity discounts to use as premiums and sales promotions, or for use in corporate training programs. To contact a representative, please e-mail us at bulksales@mcgraw-hill.com.

This book is printed on acid-free paper.

Library of Congress Cataloging-in-Publication Data

Rich, David A.
    Contagious selling : how to turn a connection into a relationship that lasts a lifetime / by David Rich.
        p. cm.
    ISBN 978-0-07-179695-8 (alk. paper)—ISBN 0-07-179695-9
(alk. paper) 1. Selling. 2. Customer relations. I. Title.
    HF5438.25.R5123 2013
    658.85—dc23   2012030631

> *I dedicated this book to the hundreds of people I have met through the years who have taught me a little something about selling and building relationships.*

Contents

	Introduction	v
CHAPTER 1	*It's a Whole New Ballgame*	1
CHAPTER 2	*The Essential Five Dynamics of Romancenomics*	15
CHAPTER 3	*Taking the Cold Out of Cold Calling*	33
CHAPTER 4	*The Art & Science of Being Contagious*	53
CHAPTER 5	*It's Not What You Say or Do; It's Who You Are*	73
CHAPTER 6	*Making a Contagious Presentation*	93
CHAPTER 7	*What's All the Fuss About Price?!*	113
CHAPTER 8	*From Captivation to Cultivation*	141
CHAPTER 9	*Cultivating Through Crisis*	159
CHAPTER 10	*The Sore-Thumb Principle*	183
	A Final Thought or Two…	201
	Index	207

Introduction

My mother-in-law can't stand the fact that her daughter married a salesman. For over 25 years, I've endured her lamentations on the obnoxiousness of salespeople. She says she can spot a salesperson from a mile away. She says they're arrogant, pushy, self-serving, manipulative, transparent, and fake. She doesn't like it when they make their "pitch," and she despises it when they try to close. It feels like high pressure to her. I think she'd rather run through the streets naked than deal with a salesperson. Her animosity runs that deep. You know what? For the most part, she's right.

I know you're thinking that I'm generalizing and condemning an entire profession because of a few bad apples. I concede the point, but too many salespeople (and more and more each day) fit my mother-in-law's preconception. It only takes a few bad apples to create a negative overall impression. Take lawyers, for example. Most lawyers are reputable and honest, but a few have been known to stretch the ethical boundaries, and that's all it took to make the general public wary and skeptical.

I may be hypersensitive to the plight of salespeople not only because I am one but also because I've been teaching selling skills for a quarter of a century. At best estimate, I've trained over a half million salespeople in my career. I don't mention this to brag as much as to set up my next point. The world has changed, and selling is a lot harder today than it's ever been. Things that worked in the past don't work today. Skills that closed the sale 30 years ago now turn customers off. Customers spot insincerity in seconds, and building relationships with them is harder than ever.

There are lots of reasons for this. For one, technology has made it harder to connect with people. Business has become a fax, a message on someone's voice mail, or an e-mail. Face-to-face meetings have become rarer with each passing year. For as much as I know better, I find myself guilty of this almost daily. I catch myself hoping to get someone's voice mail so I can quickly and effortlessly leave a message. I call this *shotgun rapport*: in and out and on to the next call. Technology may have made things speedier and easier, but it's damaging to creating and maintaining rapport and loyalty.

Another reason selling is harder is in the nature of today's economy: businesses are meaner and leaner, and they are minding the pennies closer than ever before.

Another is increased competition. When I was a kid growing up in Allentown, Pennsylvania, every male between the ages of 5 and 85 went to the same barber in town. I can remember my grandfather taking me to get my haircut from good old "Blind Charlie." Bear in mind that Charlie really wasn't blind. He earned the nickname because you couldn't get a haircut (and shave, for the older guys) without coming out bleeding. There was a joke among us kids that we could tell when someone got a haircut because we could see the scabs on the back of his neck! We didn't care. It was part of the haircut, and Charlie always gave us a bag of goodies at the end. We looked forward to it. But what would happen today if someone cut our kid's neck during a haircut? We'd be outraged at the least, and some might even pursue legal action.

Times have changed. In those days, Charlie was the only barber in town, and we got to know him well. Today, within a 5-mile radius of my house (and I live in a much smaller town than Allentown), there are at least a dozen places to get a haircut. There are 18 banks, 6 grocery stores, 8 dry cleaners, and countless places to eat. You get the picture. Competition is greater and consumers have more choices than ever before.

The biggest reason selling is harder is because buyers are more sophisticated. They have access to more information than ever before. In many cases, buyers know more about what's being sold than the salespeople.

I'll talk about this throughout the book, but suffice it to say, selling is not what it used to be. Long gone are the stereotype door-to-door sales reps who peddled their goods out of the back of their station wagon. Selling today is synonymous with relationships. A salesperson is only as good as the quality, quantity, and speed of his or her ability to build solid relationships. This can also be said of almost every profession. A business's success is directly proportional to the quality, quantity, and speed of its relationships. But it's more than just business. The same can be said of personal success.

What my mother-in-law doesn't realize is that we're all salespeople. We all have something to sell, and that's ourselves and our desires. Anyone who has ever dated another person is a salesperson. Anyone who has ever made a new friend is a salesperson. Anyone who has ever convinced another to see a particular movie or go to a certain restaurant is a salesperson. Getting married is the ultimate sale, and children are natural-born salespeople! My daughter could sell her mother and me on the idea of getting an ice cream cone just about any time she wanted one. Whether it be dating, parenting, marriage, friendships, or even casual encounters, our ability to connect to and captivate another person plays a pivotal role.

Selling is professional romance. It's about captivating another person, not on a personal level but on a professional one. If someone is arrogant, manipulative, or pushy, as my mother-in-law sees all those in selling, the relationship is dead on arrival and captivation is out of the question. But if that person is sincere, authentic, and purposeful, the relationship has a chance and a sale is possible. In short, it's about being contagious.

That's what this book is about: captivating customers and then cultivating them into genuine relationships through the power of being contagious. The dynamics of romance aren't just for lovers; they're for any relationship that needs to grow to succeed. But even being contagious can wear off if you don't continue to grow the relationship. That's where most salespeople and quite frankly most sales books and presentations fall short. Selling is not a game. It's just the beginning of a business relationship. Selling is like dating: it's only the first stage. After that, the hard work begins. Business relationships, just like personal ones, can have good moments and bad moments. They ebb and flow. They can have crises. Too often we look at selling as a transaction instead of a relationship, and that is one reason why the relationship doesn't grow beyond the sale, if even then. We aim to sell when we should be aiming to be genuinely contagious!

So if you're even remotely in the game of business relationships, fix your hair, pop a mint, settle in to your favorite reading chair, and get ready for few fresh new ideas on how to captivate customers and cultivate lasting business relationships. The basics of selling may be immutable, but how those basics are perceived and received is very different today from that of the past. I believe it's a whole new ballgame!

CHAPTER 1

It's a Whole New Ballgame

When I began selling almost 30 years ago, things were a lot different. Sure, the basics of selling are pretty much the same. I don't think the basics of being a good listener, asking good questions, making an effective presentation, and asking for the business will ever change. They are still as important as ever. There are, however, some subtle changes in selling and building relationships in the past 30 years that have changed the game significantly, with the biggest change being how much harder it is to establish and sustain a loyal relationship.

Selling is different because the world is different. Today's economy and business world are light-years from where they were when Ronald Reagan was president. Resources are more precious, and budgets are tighter. Businesses are operating leaner and meaner. We live in an increasing smaller world within a global economy. Word of mouth, both good and bad, travels farther and faster than ever before. Competition and choices for the customers are more plentiful, and businesses are smarter. However, the biggest changes in business may be with customers! Customers are more cynical, skeptical, and sophisticated, and they have access to more information than has ever been available at any point in history. All this has led to a dramatic decrease in loyalty. Customer loyalty, in all industries, is at all-time lows. At the same time, customer expectations have skyrocketed, leaving little doubt that this period in business history will come to be known as the "age of the consumer." Let me explain how we got here.

There are two major factors contributing to the rise of the consumer age. The first is the rapid rise of consumer choices. According to U.S. Bureau of Statistics, there were just shy of 11.5 million businesses that reported payroll taxes in 1992. By 2008, that number had grown to over 16.5 million, and this number doesn't even begin to record the number of online ventures and businesses that had no payroll taxes. In the small southern town where I currently live, at last count, there were 18 banks, 6 major grocery stores (not counting convenience stores), 8 dry cleaners, and hundreds of places to eat within 5 miles of my house. All this in a town of less than 18,000 people! I can't even imagine what these numbers would be in big cities, and of course, this doesn't even begin to count the uncountable number of online choices that are increasing every day. You get the picture. The days of the single-merchant towns are over. Consumers have choices they never had before, and this has raised the expectation bar. If they don't get what they want at one place, they always know there's no shortage of options.

The second, and even bigger factor, is technology. One of the reasons why there has been a huge growth in the number of businesses is that it's easier than ever to market a business. In the old days, a business would have to open its doors, maybe run an ad or two in the local newspaper, and wait for word of mouth to spread. Today, marketing begins even before the doors open, and word of mouth travels through the marketplace at unprecedented speeds. The use of technology, however, has had its biggest impact on relationships. Merchants 30 years ago had to rely on their sales reps for information. Businesses counted on those who sold them goods and services, and the reps became part of the family.

When I was a little boy, my family had close relationships with our barber, our banker, our dentist, our milkman (yes, I said milkman), and many others who sold us their wares. Today, these relationships are fragile at best. Most of us cannot even name the branch manager at our bank, let alone have a close relationship with that person. Technology has replaced the need for many relationships. Today, a merchant can conduct business online or by phone, fax, e-mail, or even text messaging. The days of the reps' strolling into their customers' business to take an order and shoot the breeze are dangerously numbered.

This reminds me of an old United Airlines commercial in which the sales manager walks into his sales meeting and announces that the company has just lost its oldest and best customer. He blames technology, stating that business has become a fax and a message on voice mail. He then tells his troops that they need to get face-to-face with all their customers again, and he hands out airline tickets to everyone. As he turns to head out of the meeting, someone yells, "Where are you going, boss?" He answers by saying he's going to pay a visit to that old customer the company had just lost.

It was a great commercial, and very prophetic. This commercial aired in the early 1990s. Today, it's even worse! Faxes are all but extinct, having been replaced by the even less personal text messages. Why call when we can text? Why visit when we can scan a document and e-mail? Why stop by and say hello when you can do it on Facebook? I speak on the importance of building relationships, yet I have caught myself hoping as the phone is ringing that I get the person's voice mail so I can leave a message or send the person a message on Facebook. This is what we've come to want these days: a quick hit, a stealth relationship, the quicker the better. Unfortunately, it's also what customers have come to want too. They don't want to wait for information, and thanks to the Internet, they don't have to. Whatever they want or need is a few clicks away. Technology has put customers in charge, and they know it. They don't have to see you to learn about your services, get a price quote, or even place an order. Relationships are optional at best. Customers are more demanding, less loyal, less patient, and less tolerant of mistakes than ever before. The toll on relationships and the selling process is undeniable. Relationships are harder to build, and customers are harder to impress.

I began selling yellow pages in 1982, and four short years later, I started my own speaking and training company. In those days, it was possible to genuinely impress a customer with good customer service and a demonstration of expertise in what we might be selling. Tom Peters's 1982 bestseller, *In Search of Excellence*, chronicled how excellence was the key to business success. If we wowed customers with our excellence, they would reward us with their business and pledge their undying loyalty. Well, that's certainly not the case today. Excellence is no longer good enough. Customers aren't "wow-able" anymore. Today, it's getting increasingly harder, if not downright impossible, to impress customers with our excellent service, dazzling product knowledge, and superior selling acumen. That's because today's customers **expect** those things. They expect excellence. They're not impressed when you deliver great service because, after all, that's what they expect and demand. And if you don't meet their expectations, they know someone else who will.

Here's a good analogy for those of you who play poker. Think of great service and superior selling skills as the ante just to stay in the hand. It doesn't mean you'll win the hand; it just puts you in the game. Great service and selling skills are the minimum requirements just to earn the right to compete. They are still very important, but they no longer give you a competitive edge in and of themselves. If businesses don't ante up to stay in the hand, the odds are overwhelmingly against them to succeed. Excellence is no longer a lofty goal to attain but rather a basic prerequisite to merely have a chance. It's a whole new ballgame, and the things that made people successful in the past will not suffice in today's ultracompetitive landscape. The bar has been raised to an unprecedented level.

So the logical next question is this: If excellence is no longer good enough, what is better than excellence? I believe the answer is "to be contagious." I know *contagious* is a strange word to use in a business context, but I think we all know what I'm talking about. We all know certain people that we were drawn to at some point in our lives. We couldn't necessarily explain why or how, but we knew we liked being in their presence.

Being contagious isn't about being the best looking, or making the most money, or being a smooth talker. It's about making a superconnection with people, often on a subconscious, unexplainable level. It can happen in a blink of an eye, or it can take years to foster. It's something that some people have, and others need to learn to develop. Either way, it's the single most important ingredient in doing business today. Being contagious applies to individual salespeople, customer service personnel, and frontline employees, managers, and leaders. Just about anyone who has contact with another person needs to understand the dynamic of being contagious. It also applies to businesses; just as a person can be contagious, so too can a business establishment. We will explore this type of contagiousness in Chapter 10. Being contagious is important for anyone, but it's absolutely essential for anyone who sells and deals with other people for a living. The selling basics may be immutable and anyone can learn them, but that means nothing if you don't understand how everything around selling has dramatically changed. Understanding this new business climate and applying selling principles to today's customer is what separates the average salesperson from the great salesperson.

Thirty years ago, selling was mechanical and somewhat predictable. It focused on completing the transaction. When I began selling, I was taught that if I had more closes than my customers had objections, I would get the sales. I was taught to close early, close often, and close hard. I was taught the ABCs of selling: Always Be Closing! My first boss taught me to memorize my presentation and start trial closing from the moment I met potential customers. I was taught to ask questions that would strategically box them into making the decision I wanted. I was taught to size up their office and surrounding décor to better analyze their likes and dislikes. I was taught that selling was a game and there were winners and losers. I was taught that "buyers were liars" and the only thing that mattered was manipulating the customers to buy what I was selling. Unbelievably, there are still many sales trainers, speakers, and authors today who continue to teach this adversarial, outdated approach. It's because sometimes, it still works. But when it does, it works only once, and it rarely leads to any kind of lasting relationship. Tricks and skills may still work, and sometimes produce sales, but they never produce long-term, loyal relationships.

Bottom line: Sales skills and techniques may help you make a sale, complete a transaction, and even meet a weekly quota, but they won't help you sustain a living. For that, you need relationships. There is no profession in the history of the world that has more turnover than selling. More people get in and more get out than is true of any other single profession. Many get into selling because there is no entrance requirement and they think selling is easy. No degree or passing a test is required. They've been told they have the gift of gab and that they are "charmers," so they become salespeople. For a while, their charm along with the ABCs, may work. But over the long term, in the absence of a genuine relationship, no customer can be counted on to be loyal beyond the transaction. Without a relationship, the loyalty is conditional and based on the transaction at hand; it is not heartfelt loyalty.

Any average salesperson can make a sale or two. Only the really great salespeople make a living selling. To sustain a career in sales, you need to have relationships, not accounts. You need to have friends, not customers. You have to remember that we are dealing with much more sophisticated customers. In most cases, the customers you are calling on know more about selling and, in some cases, know more about your product or service than you do! They've heard all the lines, and they recognize selling skills immediately. You're not the first salesperson to grace their presence. They've become savvy buyers.

When a sales technique is recognized as a sales technique, it loses its value. Sales techniques worked more effectively in the past when customers didn't recognize them, but now that they do, things are different. No one wants to be the subject and victim of technique. Old worn-out pickup lines don't work in personal relationships for the same reason. They are recognized for what they are: insincere and inappropriate. People want authenticity. They may want or even need your product or service, but they don't need you! Loyalty occurs only with a genuine relationship, and that happens only with a true, real connection.

The catch is that to foster relationships takes time, but we don't have as much time as we used to have to let our relationships build and grow. In a very few select industries, it may still be that way, but in the vast majority of today's situations, no one has the time or the inclination to foster a relationship the way they used to. You may still make a sale. In fact, you may make repeated sales. But don't confuse those sales with loyalty. There's a difference between a relationship of convenience based on a mutually beneficial transaction and a genuine relationship. Most salespeople think multiple sales and ongoing business from the same customer means there is loyalty. Don't be fooled. Today's customers will jump ship whenever a better deal comes around. Sure, you can take the easy route and always make sure you give your customer the best price and best deal, but this is a thin-ice game and almost always temporary. Sooner or later, someone always comes up with a better deal. Transactions based on convenience (which includes price) never last and never turn into real relationships.

That is why being contagious is so critical. It's the only way to sell in the age of the consumer. Today's customers don't want to be sold. They don't have the time, the patience, or the money to be manipulated by insincere salespeople just wanting to earn their commission. Today's customers have seen and heard it all. The only way to sell in today's ultracompetitive and sophisticated environment is to be so contagious that they WANT to do business with you. If two people want to do business together, they will find a way to make it happen. But if they don't, there's no magic phrase or selling technique that will make it happen.

In fact, when someone doesn't want to do business with you, you will hear a lot of excuses that aren't the real truth. You will hear things like "Your price was just too high," "I got a better deal from one of your competitors," "The project was put on hold," or "You just didn't have the right product." You will get anything but the truth that they just didn't want to do business with you. Rarely will people say "I just didn't feel comfortable with you" or "We just didn't connect."

In the absence of genuine rapport, people would rather make excuses than make it personal. There's no telling how often this occurs, but I am willing to bet that the majority of the times customers tell you that your price is too high, the price is rarely the real culprit. Citing the price is just a neutral, easy, and gentle way of brushing you off. The only way to avoid such excuses is to build genuine relationships, but that won't happen if you fail to connect. I can't say this enough: **The only way to be successful selling is to be so contagious that others want to do business with you!** With that said, the first step in being contagious is to stop looking at customers as customers and begin looking at them as people. We need to stop trying to sell and start trying to build solid relationships. To do that authentically, we need to think of selling and building business relationships in the same dynamic that exists in our personal relationships. The things that build personal, even romantic relationships are the exact same things that build any relationships. The lines between business and personal are blurred.

The lines of personal romance and business economics are intersecting in today's marketplace where it's harder than ever to build solid relationships. To be successful, we need to think about selling and customer service in different, fresher, more modern ways. We need a new paradigm, and I've created one. I call it "Romancenomics." This is the merging of the dynamics of personal romance with the immutable laws of business economics.

This is not to say that we should conduct business inappropriately or get romantically involved with our customers but rather that the principles and dynamics of romance and business are interchangeable. After all, relationships are relationships even if the goals and end results are different. We should seek to be contagious whether we are trying to make a sale, make a friend, or begin a romance. Getting an appointment and getting a date require the same chemistry and the same skill set. The goal in business may be different from that of a personal relationship, but the steps in getting there are amazingly similar.

In the next chapter, I will explore the five ways in which building a personal relationship is exactly like building a business relationship. The essential dynamics of courtship are the same whether you are selling someone professionally or romantically pursuing them. Either way, your goal is to be contagious and begin a relationship! It's personal, competitive, and emotional.

So it begins: the era of Romancenomics is here. The journey to being authentically contagious and creating a new way of doing business is beginning.

CHAPTER 2

The Essential Five Dynamics of Romancenomics

There are essentially Five Dynamics of Relationship Building that are not only identical to the dynamics of personal relationship building but are also necessary in business relationship building. I'm not necessarily suggesting that these five things are the only things that go into building great relationships, but they are the immutable essentials. If we violate any one of these, chances are the relationship will suffer. I will refer to these throughout the book, but let's look at each dynamic now as we draw the parallels of personal romance and business economics.

1. FIRST IMPRESSIONS STICK!

The first essential dynamic is obvious, but obvious for a reason: **First impressions stick!** The one thing you can never get back is a first impression. There's no re-do. Studies show that first impressions are formed within 10 seconds of meeting someone. Within those 10 seconds, people decide whether or not they want to keep moving forward, or whether they want to distance themselves. I call it the *magnetic push or pull*. There's either a push or a pull. It's a subconscious, automatic, first impression–generated reaction. They either want to move forward or pull away.

The obvious example of the magnetic pull in personal relationships is love at first sight, but more often than not, the pull isn't romantic at all. It's simply just an innocent, undetectable connection made between people. It happens millions of times every day, in person and over the telephone. In the world of selling, just as it is in romance, the presence of a pull doesn't in any way guarantee the beginning of a relationship. It just bought you a little more time. Either you've intrigued them in some way, or you haven't. The pull buys you a little time, but you have to continue to earn their attention as you go. Of course, if their first impression results in a push, you've hit a wall. It's better to end the interaction and chalk it up to poor timing rather than forge ahead. You can always try again later.

Sometimes we encounter a push because the other person is busy or distracted. There isn't a salesperson alive who hasn't called on a prospect at a bad time. If it truly is a bad time, you will undoubtedly get a push. Recognize it for what it is, and offer to contact the person somewhere down the road. The prospect will appreciate your sensitivity, and even though you haven't gained anything, you haven't permanently damaged the relationship either. Forging your way through a push can be fatal to any future relationship prospects. I will explore ways to make a favorable first impression in the next chapter, but for now, understand that people's first impressions stick!

2. IT'S ALL ABOUT FEELING

The second essential dynamic is that **it's all about feeling**. It's not what you know or what the facts are. It's about the emotion. It's about how one feels. Relationships are not statistical. They are emotional. In marketing classes all over the country, students are taught about the Eureka factor. The Eureka factor states that people make decisions based on subjective experience, but they validate their decisions with logic. To put it in plainer English, people make decisions based on emotion and feeling, but they use logic and hard data to justify their decision. The word *eureka* is Greek, and it means "I have found it," so some people also describe the Eureka factor as "the sudden or illuminating flash of enlightenment" used in decision making. It's when you find the answer or see the light. It can be an "aha" moment or the gut feeling that something "feels" right. It's the realization of emotion, yet it is way too touchy-feely to be verbalized. So we justify and verbalize our decisions with logic, data, or hard evidence.

There are, of course, many factors that play into an emotional decision. Many will be explored in later chapters, but there are two general factors that must be present from the first moment of contact. They are *confidence* and *presence*. I am often asked to define what makes a person contagious. It's a tough question because there are so many things that contribute to it, and it's hard to define without a lengthy explanation. However, if I had to pin down my answer as to what makes someone contagious in a few words, it would confidence and presence! Both are equally essential, and neither can be faked. Either you have them or you don't.

Confidence is not arrogance or conceit. Nor is confidence necessarily bold and obvious. Confidence is the quiet assurance that one believes in who he or she is and feels comfortable in his or her own skin. It is manifested by a look in people's eyes, a bounce in their step, or tone in their voice. Confidence doesn't mean that people always have all the answers or that they never second-guess themselves. It simply means they believe in themselves and in what they are doing. Confidence is contagious because it is a rare commodity. We're naturally drawn to people who are confident because we feed off their energy and it inspires hope. We admire confidence personally, but the marketplace also follows suit and rewards confidence.

Would you be impressed to learn that in 1976 Steve Jobs and his partner sold their Volkswagen van to get a few bucks to build the first Apple personal computer in his garage? Did you know Michael Dell began selling computer components from his college dorm room and later dropped out to sell full time? Did you know that Philip Knight and his college track coach sold imported Japanese track shoes from the trunk of his station wagon? Those were the humble beginnings of Apple, Dell Computer, and Nike. What all three had in common was vision and confidence. Perhaps it was their vision that gave them confidence, or maybe it was the confidence that gave them the vision, but either way, they believed in themselves.

The other general factor in an emotional decision is presence. Presence is much harder to define but just as easy to spot. Presence is the aura and energy that surrounds you that cannot be seen but definitely can be experienced. We all know people with amazing presence. We notice when they walk into a room—not because they announce their arrival but rather because they exude positive vibes. We subconsciously crave to be around people with presence. Of course, they are confident, but it's more than just that. They are inspiring. They see the glass as always being half full, they can smile even if they don't always feel happy, and they are accountable to themselves. They don't blame the weather, the economy, their upbringing, or anything outside of themselves for their station in life. They are who they are. And where they are and where they are going are all their own doing. They have no regrets. They create a life rather than letting life create them. Presence, like confidence, is contagious because it is a quality we all admire but very few of us possess. The good news is that if I haven't been describing you, it's not too late. You can develop these qualities.

There are many things that can help you develop confidence and presence. Commitment to ongoing learning and development is one thing. I often say that I can tell how successful someone is by how many books they have read in the past three years. The average person doesn't even complete a single book in one year! Successful people know that continued learning is paramount for getting and staying ahead in a competitive world.

Harry Truman once said, "Not all readers are leaders, but all leaders are readers!" Learning is the ultimate competitive advantage. I have spent the last 25 years helping companies build better sales and customer service operations and reputations, and what always amazes me is the lack of commitment to learning that most organizations have. Too often learning is seen as an event instead of a process. As a speaker, I've always enjoyed being part of an event, but the event is a small step in the process, not the end of the road. There are so many great quotes out there about the importance of learning, but my all time favorite is one from legendary author and speaker Zig Ziglar. He once said, "The only thing worse than training your people and losing them is not training them and keeping them."

Learning is not a luxury. It is an outright necessity if you want to compete. If your company is a believer in ongoing learning and education, be thankful and embrace as much as the company will offer. However, learning is not necessarily the responsibility of your company. It is YOUR responsibility. When I interview potential salespeople, I often ask them to give me some of the titles in their personal development library. If they give me a blank stare as if I've asked some ridiculous, obscure question, the interview rarely continues. Think about it this way: If you are not willing to invest in yourself, why should any employer? Learning is your responsibility, not your company's. Now I admit I am more than likely preaching to the choir since you have purchased and are reading this book. My hope is that if you are not a habitual learner, you will become one.

However, the single greatest contributor to confidence and presence is passion and conviction for what you do. I'll explore the quality of conviction a bit more in depth in Chapter 4, but there is a big difference between liking what you do and loving it. I once read that 97 percent of all working Americans would quit their jobs if they won $10 million in the lottery. That tells me a lot of things, but one of them is that most people work only to get paid. If they stop getting paid or they don't need to get paid, then there's no more need for the job. How sad!

I grew up (and still am) a huge baseball fan. I grew up watching greats like Pete Rose, Roberto Clemente, and later Cal Ripken and Kirk Gibson play. They played with such passion that it was obvious to everyone how much they loved the game. Unfortunately, most of the players today seem to lack this passion. In interviews, the talk of loving to play is replaced by how it's a business and why the player needs to make even more money.

Now don't misunderstand me. I am all for making money. However, making money should always be a benefit, not a prerequisite. I have always subscribed to the theory that if you love what you do, you'll never work another day in your life. Players should love playing first, and making money second, but sadly it is the other way around, and it is obvious to us fans. It's also obvious to customers. Sure, it's easy to bash multimillionaire athletes, but what about you? Are you doing what you're doing only because you get a paycheck? Are you perhaps guilty of the same thinking as that of today's professional athletes? Are you working only for the money? Are you selling for a living merely because you have a talent for it? I hope not. I hope you make a lot of money, but if you lose the passion for selling what you sell, your feelings will always be obvious to your customers just as the lack of the players' passion is obvious to those who watch sports.

Customers buy you and your conviction first, your product or service second. There is nothing more contagious than people who love what they do and feel a true sense of purpose for doing it. Your customers may not be able to articulate it, but they will feel drawn to do business with you. Passion is the ultimate *magnetic pull*. Passion is far more persuasive and responsible for more sales than any brochure, PowerPoint presentation, or eloquent proposal ever has been. The light that shines in your eye that tells customers that you love what you do and believe deeply that your product or service can make a difference in their life is far more compelling than anything you might say.

If you get nothing out of this book other than learning how to, or rediscovering how to, love selling, you will greatly benefit. Start by asking yourself why you're doing what you're doing. List what you love about selling and what you don't like about it. Chances are you love the same things we all love about selling. We love the variety, and we love how every day is different and brings new people and challenges into our lives. We love the freedom, and we love that we are not tied to office chairs and we can get out into the world every day. We love the opportunity, and we love that we can be as successful as we choose to be. We love the thrill of the sale and the feeling we get when we land a big deal. Selling is like no other profession in the world. Fall in love with it and you will find that selling will fall in love with you.

3. ORDER MATTERS

The third essential dynamic is that **order matters**. Just as in any personal relationship, there is an unspoken timetable to any sale. Violate the order and your chances of making the sale decrease dramatically. Allow me to draw some parallels between personal and professional relationship building that you might relate to.

Let's say you are on a first date. You are no more than 10 minutes into the date and your date asks you a very intimate, personal question. What is your likely reaction? The odds are good that you are taken aback and even offended. But think about why you are offended. You're not offended just because your date asked you a personal question. You fully expect to share more and more personal information as the weeks and months of a relationship wear on. You're offended at the timing! The personal question was too soon. It was out of order.

There is a rhythm to any and all successful relationships, and violating this rhythm, intentionally or unintentionally, will always cause tension. The best way to respond to a personal question asked out of order is to keep it light and let the other person know there is a time and place for that question but that time is not now. Similarly, in selling situations, often prospective customers will ask a question out of order. They will ask about your price almost before they get your name. Perhaps they do it to throw you off your game, or they are trying to save time by cutting to the chase, or maybe it's just because everyone is super–price conscious these days. Whatever the reason, it's a rhythm altering question. It's a fair question, and one you will eventually have to answer, but at this moment, the question's out of order.

I will address this more specifically in Chapter 7, but suffice it to say, how you answer that question will determine if the relationship has any shot of progressing. You do not want to give any prices or price ranges. You want to let customers know that you are more than eager to get to that part of the relationship, but you're not there yet. There are many clever ways of doing this, but my all-time favorite is to say, "I will answer that more specifically later, but we're not the cheapest nor are we the most expensive. However, if we are not 100 percent right for you, there won't be any charge at all." I must confess that it is not a David Rich original, but it's a perfect answer. It gently implies that if your product or service is not right for them, you won't be doing business together, and that means there is no cost to them. It's a way of answering without answering, but it keeps the relationship moving forward.

There are many other examples of how getting out of order can impact a relationship, and we will uncover them as we move through the sales process throughout this book, but always keep in mind that order does indeed matter!

4. IF YOU HAVE TO CLOSE, SOMETHING WENT WRONG

The fourth essential dynamic is that **if you have to close, something went wrong**. I know that goes against everything you've probably been taught from day one of your selling career. You've undoubtedly been taught to "close early and often," and you've been given the ABCs of selling: Always Be Closing. However, this is not the best way to sell in today's seen-it-all, sophisticated marketplace.

A closing should be nothing more than a gentle nudge when the time is right. It should not be a tactic to manipulate another person. If more than a gentle nudge is needed, you shouldn't even think about closing. Put having to close through the filter of a personal relationship. If someone has to close, then there probably isn't very good natural chemistry. Rarely does someone ask to kiss another person. When it's right, it just happens. Both parties are in agreement and are in unison. They know from a look or a gesture when the timing feels right. Same is true in business.

A closing should be like a first kiss. It should be the natural next step in the progression of a relationship. You should never close if you are not absolutely certain the answer is YES, just as you never want to lean into that kiss and get rebuffed. If you're not certain, trust your instincts. It's probably not the right time to even attempt it. To always be closing means that you're always trying to force the timing and you'll more than likely get rejected a lot. I like to teach my own version of ABC with a second C: Always Be Captivating & Cultivating. If you think of customers and potential customers in terms of always wanting to captivate them and then cultivating the relationship with them, you will be perceived as being more genuine, and you will avoid many of the pitfalls that doom a relationship. Timing is everything, and if you have to close, something went dreadfully wrong.

5. IT'S NEVER OVER

The fifth and last essential dynamic is that **it's never over**. Way too often, salespeople think of selling as having a beginning and an ending. The beginning is the first contact, and the ending is the sale. Great salespeople know that selling never ends. Selling is not a line. It is a circle that keeps going round and round. You want to keep building and cultivating the relationship, hopefully forever! Relationships unfortunately do have endings sometimes, but you do not want that to ever happen. Relationships have endings more often than not because someone saw it as a transaction that had a beginning and an end rather than as an ongoing process.

I am friends with and still have relationships with some of my customers long after they've changed jobs and even retired! I don't get any business from them anymore, but we still have the relationship. In fact, in many cases, it's also still profitable for me. Every now and then,

I get a referral from an old friend even though it's been years since we've actually done business together. The circle never ends if you see it that way.

One of the best ways to change the way you see your professional relationships is to shift the goal. Instead of centering the goal on sales or transactions, shift the goal to establishing relationships. If you don't do this, and if you allow the sale to become your sole focus, your goal will become apparent to the customers, which will make trust all the harder to create. It should be relationship first, sale second, not the other way around. Making a sale will be the result of having created trust and solid connections.

Think of it this way: in a personal relationship when someone perceives the other person's motive to be self-serving, that perception severely handicaps any chance of there being any real, long-lasting relationship between them. We've all met people who we immediately felt weren't truly interested in us—people who were interested only in what they could get out of us. Those people were focused on transactions instead of relationships.

~

We will explore these dynamics further in later chapters, but for now: make selling personal. For years I have raised lots of eyebrows in my seminars when I say that the best way to sell to a twenty-first-century customer is to NOT sell at all. *Selling* implies a wrong connotation. Instead, the best way to sell is to build relationships. Have fun, be authentic, and make friends. When you do that, you will become contagious, and being contagious will yield you more sales than you could ever imagine.

CHAPTER 3

Taking the Cold Out of Cold Calling

In any relationship, the most important moment is the very first time you have any type of contact with the other person. The reason this moment is so important has already been stated, and that's because first impressions stick. However, it's more than just the fact that they stick. First impressions are the single biggest opportunity to be contagious. In a personal relationship, you want sparks to fly. In a business relationship, you don't necessarily want the same kind of sparks to fly, but you do want to capture the person's interest. You want sparks of interest instead of sparks of romance but sparks nonetheless.

We live in an age when attention spans are short and the window to pique people's interest is as short as it's ever been. In this chapter, we will explore the ways to make those first initial contacts with prospective customers and how to be contagious from those very important first few moments. Most salespeople dread this initial prospecting stage, but it's a golden opportunity to immediately connect, and if done properly, it can be extremely fun and exciting. In this chapter we will learn how to take the cold out of cold calling!

GETTING PREPARED TO BEGIN A NEW RELATIONSHIP

Before we get into the actual contact phase, we must first make sure that we are fully prepared and ready to begin a new relationship. This may be surprising, but it happens frequently: many salespeople simply pick up the phone or walk into a customer's place of business prematurely, without any forethought or preparation. That's about as cold as a cold call can get. It needs to be warmed up a bit. I am not suggesting that you need to spend hours researching your prospect before you make contact, although the rule of thumb is that the bigger the price tag, the more preparation is needed. If you are selling office supplies, you may not need as much research as you would if you were selling a customized motor coach, but no matter what you sell, there's always some prep work.

As a bare minimum, you need to make sure that you are psychologically ready to sell. I certainly don't want to turn into Sigmund Freud here, but selling is mostly mental. Are you enthusiastic and positive, and are you ready to show those feelings to customers? Are you ready to handle rejection? Do you have goals? Have you mapped out your day, week, and month? Do you have a plan? The answers to these questions take mental preparation, and they must be answered before you are anywhere near ready to make contact with customers. Let's go through each question briefly.

Are You Enthusiastic and Positive?

The need for enthusiasm seems so obvious and elementary, yet thousands of salespeople hit the streets every day with a less than excited and motivated attitude. Zig Ziglar once said, "Selling is a transfer of enthusiasm." Plainly and simply put, you can't transfer what you don't have. If you want other people to get excited about your product or service, you must first get excited about it yourself. Many call this the *law of excitement*. Whatever you get excited about will in turn get excited about you. The key to this is that you must get excited first.

Average salespeople get excited AFTER they've made a sale. Great sales people get excited first. It's easy to get excited about selling after you make a sale, but to be great, you must understand that excitement is not the result of the sale. It is the cause of the sale. Being enthusiastic and genuinely excited is a major contributor to making the sale in the first place.

I don't think this is the kind of thing that can be measured by a statistic, but I am willing to bet that an enthusiastic, positive attitude helps increase the likelihood of establishing any kind of relationship tenfold!

Are You Able to Handle Rejection?

This part of the mental preparation is a bit trickier. No matter how much we think we're able to handle rejection, it's always harder than we imagine. We're humans with egos and feelings. No one likes to be rejected, yet it is an inevitable and unavoidable part of professional selling. In fact, more people will say no than will say yes. There are a couple really good ideas for preparing for and handling rejection.

The first is to always remember that the prospects are not rejecting you. Do not take it personally. Most rejection happens simply because the timing isn't right. You may have caught them in the middle of a really stressing situation, or perhaps they are preoccupied with something personal going on in their lives. Maybe they just received bad news, or maybe they were running out the door as you called. There are countless reasons why you may get rejected that have absolutely nothing to do with you or what you're selling. It's just bad timing.

The second idea about rejection is to make it a game. Tell yourself that every rejection brings you that much closer to a yes. When I was selling yellow page advertising many moons ago, I used to employ a technique that was very helpful in dealing with rejection. Whenever I would get turned down, upon immediately returning to the private confines of my car, I would shout out at the top of my lungs: "NEXT!" I know there were times that I shouted so loudly that others could hear, but I didn't care. I was programming my mind that I had to get through that rejection to get to the next customer who might say yes. For me, it was a display of letting go of what had just taken place and eagerly looking forward to what was yet to come. "NEXT!" became my daily mantra, and it helped me through many difficult days.

Do You Have Goals?

The third question is this: Do you have goals? Sadly, most salespeople don't. They may have quotas that were thrust upon them by someone else, but they don't have goals. Goals are highly personal. They are separate from quotas and company mandated targets. Goals don't come from someone else. They are yours and yours alone. Goals are also highly specific. A goal to succeed or to be happy is a great thought but a bad goal. It is not measurable and it is not specific enough.

Have You Mapped out Your Day, Week, and Month?

Another major criterion for a goal is that it must be broken down into its smallest denominators. That's one of the reasons why I never suggest you set as a goal how much money you want to make. It's too big. It needs to broken down into daily activities.

Instead of setting a goal based on how much money you want to make, take the income you want and work backward. For instance, figure out how many sales you need to make based on the commissions you are paid, and then work backward. Dale Carnegie used to say that the average salesperson would have to contact 50 people to get 10 appointments to make two sales.

I am not suggesting that those will be your numbers. The important thing is to figure out what your numbers will be. If you need 100 sales (based on your average sales amount) to hit your income target, how many appointments do you need to make those 100 sales? If your number is 300, then you'll need to know how many contacts you'll need to make to get those 300 appointments.

Let's say your number is 900. Then your formula would be 900 contacts to get 300 appointments to get 100 sales (900 → 300 → 100). Fortunately or unfortunately, Dale Carnegie lived in a day and age before cell phones and e-mails. Today's customers use those luxuries of technology to screen calls, and while it might be easier to make contact with people, it's much harder to really connect. So we need to add one more number to the equation, the number of contact attempts. You might need to dial or e-mail prospects several times before you actually get a chance to talk to them.

You'll need to figure out how many attempts you need to make to actually contact your prospects. Let's say, for example's sake, that your number is 1,800. That means you need to attempt 1,800 times to actually talk to 900 decision makers to set 300 appointments to make 100 sales! You may need to collect data for at least six weeks before you have enough of a sampling to base your calculations on, but once you have it, you'll have a solid formula to base your goals on.

It's not enough to set as a goal how much money you want to make, That goal is too vague. You don't have direct control over that. The only number in the entire formula that you have direct control over is how many attempts you'll make. You can't wake up in the morning and go make a sale 100 percent of the time. You can do that sometimes but not often enough to count on it. But you can wake up in the morning and make a phone call 100 percent of the time. That's where your goal needs to be. If you need 1,800 attempts, break it down into monthly, weekly, and daily numbers. So 1,800 attempts are 150 per month, 37.5 per week, and 7.5 per day. Making 7.5 attempts each day is your goal because that is the number you can control.

Having measurable goals is very empowering and motivating because if you meet the goals, you will definitely reach your income targets. It's simple arithmetic.

Do You Have a Plan?

There are really only two reasons why sales-people don't make the kind of money they want to make: either they never took the time to figure out their individual formula, or they didn't make the necessary number of contact attempts each and every day.

If it sounds simple, it is. It's not easy, but it really is that simple. Set as your goal the daily number of contact attempts you need to make each day, and then make sure you consistently hit that number. Map out each week so you have enough prospects to call. Every salesperson will have different ratios and different sets of numbers, but if you plan the work and work the plan, you will hit your goals!

INITIATING CONTACT

Once you are psychologically ready to sell, you are ready to initiate contact. Thanks to emerging technologies, there are countless ways to initiate contact these days, but the main three are by phone, in person, or by mail, either standard or e-mail. There are pros and cons of each. Mail and e-mail are efficient and easy, but they yield the lowest results. In person is time-consuming and physically demanding, but it yields the best results. In terms of ease of contact and results, the phone splits the difference between the two.

Rather than dissect the mechanics of the contact, I want to focus on how you can be contagious, regardless of the way you choose to contact new potential customers. Whether by phone, e-mail, or in person, you must have a sense of purpose, be able to display confidence, and capture the prospects' attention within seconds. I call these precious seconds the most important moment because it determines whether or not the relationship has a chance to succeed. For that reason, I have also been known to call it the Gatekeeper Moment. This is the moment "contagious" happens or doesn't happen. This moment can open the door, or even close it forever.

This moment consists of the *words you say*, *how you say them*, and *how you look when you're saying them*. In this moment, your words must be clear yet concise, your demeanor must be confident yet at ease, and your voice must command attention yet show a little humility. At first blush, these may sound a bit contradictory, but they are not at all. It may be paradoxical, but it is absolutely possible to display all of those qualities through any and all of the methods of contact. It's the delicate combination of these qualities that make you contagious!

The first hurdle is to get past the actual gatekeeper. There are many sales trainers that teach tricks and gimmicks to avoid gatekeeper scrutiny. I do not. I believe the gatekeeper is someone you must (and should want to) build a relationship with. Be humble and appeal for the gatekeeper's help. I like to tell the gatekeepers right up front that I need their help getting in touch with the person I need to reach. Do not speak down to them, and apply the same rules we just discussed. Contagious sells. Once you get past the gatekeeper and reach your contact person, the romance begins in earnest.

INTEREST QUESTIONS

Although the words you say may be less influential than the tone of your voice and your body language, they are nevertheless crucial. They must be straight to the point and contain something that captures the prospects' attention. Most salespeople make the fatal mistake of prospecting from their own point of view. They say things like "I'd like to take a few minutes of your time to show you how I can save you money" or "I'd like to introduce my company to you." These statements may be easy and straight to the point, but your prospects don't care about what you'd like to do. We need to build trust a little slower and prospect from their point of view.

While there may be countless ideas, methods, and scripts for the words you say when prospecting for new business, I believe the very best at prospecting from the customers' point of view is something I call the "Interest Question," or IQ for short. I have been teaching sales people the IQ for over 20 years, and I am happy to report that it's been time and battle tested. The IQ consists of six steps: The Greeting, The Reason, The Connection, The Problem, The Question, and The Icing.

Step 1. The Greeting

The Greeting is easy, and it's already something we do with great mastery. It's simply identifying yourself and your company. You can't initiate contact with another person without this being the first words. "Hi, my name is John Doe with John Doe & Associates" is all that's needed in a perfect greeting. However, if the name of your company does not clearly give the prospects an idea as to what your company does, a very brief second line of description is also necessary. For example, "Hi, my name is John Doe with John Doe & Associates. We conduct customized sales training programs that produce guaranteed results."

Step 2. The Reason

The Reason is an acknowledgment of your interruption and of your very good reason for doing so. "I know I may have caught you in the middle of something, but the reason I wanted to catch you is _____." Those are the words, but as with all words, the magic is in how you say them. I'll get to that in a bit, but the emphasis must be on the word "reason."

Step 3. The Connection

The Connection is the part of the IQ that tells the prospects that you have some experience in dealing with others in a similar industry or capacity. It's the part of the IQ that connects the dots between being someone they don't know interrupting their day to being someone they have a mutually beneficial and prosperous relationship with. It fills in the blank from the previous section. It goes like this: "I know I may have caught you in the middle of something, but the reason I wanted to catch you is that through my experiences working with other sales managers and executives, one of the things they've been telling me is _____."

This does a couple very important things. First, it lets them know that you have experience working with people like them, and second, it peaks their curiosity. You're not talking about *you* think; you're talking about what other sales managers think! The more specific you are with it, the more effective it will be.

Instead of saying, "In my experience working with other sales managers," you might say, "In my experience working with other sales managers for over 12 years" or "In my experience working with other sales managers in the office products industry."

The more specific to them, the better, but ultimately who do you think is more influential to them at this stage of the relationship: you or their peers? Of course, it's their peers. They want to know what their peers said. They want to know what you know. They want to either validate or invalidate what you might say next. Their curiosity may not lead to a relationship, but it will allow you to keep going!

Step 4. The Problem

The Problem is the heart of the IQ. It's a continuation of the previous sections and the part that ultimately hooks them. It takes a bit of forethought and preparation. The million dollar question you must answer prior to initiating any form of contact is this: What might be the potential problem they are having that you can help with? If you don't have an answer to that question, don't even think of contacting prospective customers. Even if you aren't sure of your answer, it is critical that you have one. After all, it isn't you who is suggesting they have the problem; it's their peers.

The problem you state should be a result of your experience or at least knowledge gained from working with others in their industry or similar profession. If you haven't actually worked with other people in their industry and you have no direct knowledge yourself, ask around the office. Ask your sales manager and other reps in your company. If you don't have the personal experience, leverage the experience of others. Do a little homework if necessary, but attempt to come up with a credible problem that the prospects might have that you might be able to help with.

Let's continue with our example:

> I know I may have caught you in the middle of something, but the reason I wanted to catch you is that in my experience working with other sales managers for over 12 years, one of the things they've been telling me is that when times get tough and money gets tight, sales education usually ends up taking the back seat and sales reps too often fall back on bad habits and old techniques.

Notice how I stated the problem. I didn't just superficially gloss over it. I went into a bit of detail. What I want to happen is for the prospects to say or think to themselves, "That's right. I do have that problem." So the more specific I can be, the better the chances of that happening.

Step 5. The Question

The next step is The Question. This is nothing more than asking for something. Ask for whatever you want to happen next. More than likely, this is a face-to-face meeting or a scheduled next telephone conversation. This step is simple, and no one ever gets it wrong.

The problem is that most salespeople skip all the steps between the greeting and the question. They say, "Hi, my name is John Doe with John Doe & Associates. We conduct customized sales training programs that produce guaranteed results. I was hoping you and I could get together for a few minutes sometime over the next week or two."

In this example, the sales rep went from step 1 straight to step 5. He bypassed all the important stuff that influences and connects with another person. This is one-sided prospecting. It's prospecting from the salesperson's point of view instead of from the customer's point of view, and it happens all the time. The Question is an important step. You must ask for what you want, but only after you've built your case and have your prospects' attention if you want them to consider granting your request.

Step 6. The Icing

The final step is The Icing. This is just what it sounds like. You've got their attention, you've connected with them through the problem, and you've asked for a meeting. The sixth step cements their decision by ending with a benefit. I like to use what I call a *double-barreled benefit*. A benefit is what your product or service will do for them.

EXAMPLE OF A WELL-CRAFTED INTEREST QUESTION

Let's put the entire IQ together:

> Hi, my name is John Doe with John Doe & Associates. We conduct customized sales training programs that produce guaranteed results. I know I may have caught you in the middle of something, but the reason I wanted to catch you is that in my experience working with other sales managers

for over 12 years, one of the things they've been telling me is that when times get tough and money gets tight, sales education usually ends up taking the back seat and sales reps too often fall back on bad habits and old techniques. I was wondering if you had 15 minutes sometime this week to get together so I can show you how our customized educational presentations can not only help you increase sales but serve as a motivational shot in the arm as well.

That is a well-crafted IQ. Each step is designed to keep the prospects engaged enough to get to the next step. I am not asking for them to make a sales decision or spend any money. The only decision I am asking for is whether they can give me 15 minutes face-to-face.

GENERAL NOTES ON USING INTEREST QUESTIONS

The IP technique works, but I warn you, it will not flow trippingly off your tongue. The first few times you use it, you will more than likely hang up the phone thinking it was too long and cumbersome. It just takes practice. The magic of the IQ is not in the words but rather in how you say them. Just as seasoned actors make reciting their script sound natural and off the cuff, good salespeople make their IQ sound the same way. If your IQ sounds memorized or scripted, it will not work.

You should have several IQs. Each industry and job type you call on should have a separate IQ. The one above is for sales managers, but I have different one when I am calling on customer service managers and executives.

The key, again, is to sound natural. This means you can't be reading off a piece of paper. Over the telephone, how you say the words trumps the words themselves, so make sure you practice the IQ until you know it frontward and backward. Then, and only then, are you ready to call prospects.

If you are walking into your prospects' place of business, you also don't want to be reading the IQ off a piece of paper. You want to be humble for interrupting them yet assertive, confident and straight to the point.

When walking in, your body language trumps both the words and how you sound. It is imperative that you look the part of a confident, sincere, naturally sounding professional.

Make sure you make good direct eye contact, and always extend your hand for a handshake first.

One of the biggest myths about handshakes is that a man must wait for a woman to extend her hand first or that a man should shake a woman's hand differently from the way he shakes a man's hand. The truth is that a handshake, at least in America, is a gender-neutral form of communication. Generally, a handshake that is too hard for a woman is also too hard for a man. A handshake is not a show of strength. A handshake should be firm, but the knuckles shouldn't bend back or turn white. I can't tell you how many women have told me that they made a decision not to do business with someone because he or she didn't know how to shake their hand. It may be a small thing, but small things matter.

I will tackle the subjects of voice and body language more deeply in the next chapter, but make no mistake: the very first words you say and how you say them and how you look when you say them together make up the most important moment you will ever have with a customer. You can't have a relationship with someone if it never begins.

Getting the chance to sell is the first step to selling. You can't steal second base if you don't get on first. You have to capture the prospects' attention and spark their interest from the moment your eyes or voices meet. It's the first opportunity you have to be contagious. Make the most of it.

CHAPTER 4

The Art & Science of Being Contagious

In this chapter, we will look closer at the science of the spoken word and body language and the role they play in being contagious. In other words, it's the science of how you sound and how you look, the vocal and the visual.

There are many conflicting statistics on how words, sounds, and visual cues are broken out in terms of what is most persuasive when you are communicating with other people, but most fall in the neighborhood of around 7 percent for the actual words you say, 38 percent for the way you sound, and 55 percent for the way you look. I've already given what I believe are the absolute best words to use when first contacting a prospect, so let's pick up where we left off and look more closely at the vocal and visual qualities that make us contagious.

We've already explored how business relationships mirror personal relationships. The same dynamics apply to any kind of connection. In advertising circles, the same model is taught as *attention, interest, desire, and action* (AIDA). Any good advertising takes the potential customer through those steps, in order. Missing a step or getting a step out of order can jeopardize the entire process. The same is true in selling, making friends, or romance. You must get someone's attention first, then spark interest, create desire, and stimulate action. It's universal and just that simple. It's not easy, but it is that simple.

THE SCIENCE OF SOUND: PARALINGUISTICS

The words we use in selling are vital in getting propects' attention, but it is the vocal and visual cues that come into play to spark their interest. Just as in any personal relationship, it's the little, seemingly undetectable things that spark interest—a glance, a look, a movement, and a tone in our voice. The science of the sound of our voice is not new. It is often referred to as *paralinguistics*, and it is taught in many schools and universities across the country in inter-personal communication courses. There are also many books written on this subject alone, and to cover it completely would take an entire book. However, it is important that we cover at least the basics because the sound of our voice conveys such incredible emotional and subconscious signals that spark interest.

Vocal Patterns

Basically, there are four primary vocal patterns but only two primary ways of measuring sound: *rate* and *inflection*. For simplicity, I've always referred to the four as SRHI, SRLI, FRLI, and FRHI. As you can guess, the first letter in each abbreviation indicates the rate of speech, and the third letter indicates inflection.

Slow Rate/High Inflection (SRHI) Speakers

These are people who talk at a slow to normal rate and are characterized by a casual, relaxed demeanor with very warm gestures and friendly overtones. They also have a lot of inflection in their voice and exhibit openness with their body language. They smile readily and tend to wear all their emotions on their sleeve. They are easy to talk to and get to know, and if they like you, they will be easy to become friends with. They are better listeners than talkers. They tend to be very attentive and loyal, but they also expect the same kind of attention and loyalty from you. For this reason, they can be very high maintenance customers. The thing that's most important to them is feelings. They want to like you and you to like them. They take their time with decisions until they feel comfortable with you.

Slow Rate/Low Inflection (SRLI) Speakers

These people talk at a slow to normal rate but are much more deliberate and mechanical with their tone, gestures, and body language than SRHI speakers. It's as if everything they say is well thought out. They are generally not comfortable in networking situations, and they avoid speaking to large groups. They are accurate and analytical, and they demand accuracy and timeliness from you. They are guarded with their expressions and share information only on a need-to-know basis. For this reason, they are tough to get to know and connect with. The things that are most important to them are data and details. They never make quick, gut decisions. In fact, they are slow and methodical decision makers. They want to know that you've done your homework, and they like everything to be in writing.

Fast Rate/Low Inflection (FRLI) Speakers

These are people who talk at a normal to high rate but with a low degree of inflection. They come across as authoritative and direct. They do not exhibit a lot of facial gestures or animation, and they like people who get straight to the point, go to the bottom line, and don't waste time. They often answer questions with one-word answers, and they get impatient if you aren't succinct enough. The most important thing to them is time. While they can be quick decision makers, you rarely know where you stand with them. They resist allowing you to get too close to them, and they prefer to correspond by e-mail and quick voice-mail messages.

Fast Rate/High Inflection (FRHI) Speakers

These are people who talk at a normal to fast rate but with a high degree of inflection and a liberal use of body language and animated facial gestures. They are known as the life of the party, and they have no trouble initiating conversation with just about anyone. They are better talkers than listeners. They have short attention spans if they are not engaged and interested. They make quick decisions and often overlook the details. The most important thing to them is energy. They like high-energy, fun people, and they tend to be eternal optimists and highly romantic. However, they get bored easily, and for this reason they tend to not be very loyal. They are susceptible to the flavor of the week and the next sweet-talking salesperson that walks in their door.

Recognizing People's Vocal Patterns

So, how is all this relevant? Well, first off, recognizing someone's vocal pattern is not an exercise in personality typing. Even though I gave some representative personality characteristics with each pattern, every one of us uses all four patterns. We may have a dominant pattern, but it is common (and quite natural) to exhibit different patterns depending on who we're with, the circumstances, and the environment. I may naturally be an FRHI speaker, but on Sunday afternoons, it's amazing how SRHI I become. Then again, if I am stressed under pressure, I become an FRLI speaker. Yet in other situations I may be an SRLI speaker. All of us are all four patterns.

The magic is not in labeling people but in recognizing where they are at a particular moment in time and to meet them where they are. Some call it *mirroring* or *style flexing*, but I simply call it *being sensitive*. I may like to interact with FRHI speakers, but if the person I am selling to is an SRLI speaker, we will only clash if I am not sensitive to the way he or she is communicating.

To truly be good at this, you must alter your definition of the Golden Rule. The biblical Golden Rule that our mom and dad taught us says, "Do unto others as you would have them do unto you." In other words, treat others the way we would like to be treated. This is great in theory, and I am certainly not finding fault with the spirit of this timeless wisdom. However, in practical relationship building, the Golden Rule has its flaws. If I am truly living by the Golden Rule, I will treat everyone as I want to be treated. I will do business with people the way I want to do business. I will interact with customers the way I want to be interacted with.

The flaw is that not everyone will want to be treated the way I want to be treated. Not everyone will want to do business the same way I do, and not everyone will want to be interacted with the way I like to interact. In selling, we need a new Golden Rule: "Do unto others the way they want to be done unto." It sounds corny, but it is sound advice.

Be sensitive, and interact with other people not according to your preferences but according to theirs. By quickly recognizing the vocal pattern in which they are communicating, you can, and should, set aside your preferred vocal pattern and match theirs. Since we've already established that all of us use all four patterns, this is not fake or manipulative. It is simply being sensitive by showing the side of you that matches the side they are showing. It's getting in step with other people. It's getting on other people's wavelength. It's what occurs naturally and subconsciously whenever two people really "click" and hit it off. By recognizing and being sensitive to another person's vocal patterns, you can be contagious by choice rather than by chance!

THE ELEMENTS OF PRESENCE

The visual aspect of contagiousness is even more complicated. There are visual aspects about our appearance, our body language, our environment, and our physical presentation. Put all of these aspects together and they make up something called our *presence*. If you're not sure what I mean by that, that's OK. It's a hard quality to describe but an easy quality to recognize. The *Merriam-Webster Collegiate Dictionary* lists the following definition of *presence:* "A noteworthy quality of poise and effectiveness." It's that intangible quality that makes people notice and admire you. It's that "larger-than-life" quality. It's unmistakable and highly contagious. There are many elements that contribute to someone's having presence, but I will focus on what I believe are the top three.

Conviction

The first one is *conviction*: not contrived, temporary, or event-driven conviction but real conviction that you believe in what you're doing and what you sell. Real conviction can't be faked, and it always shows, or doesn't show, through your eyes! That's right, your eyes. There is NO greater sales tool than your eyes. Conversely, there is no greater detriment to selling than your eyes as well. Your eyes say more to a customer than your words ever will. Among the things your eyes show are confidence, commitment, belief, passion, sincerity, integrity, humility, honesty, and willingness to serve. People make subconscious, split-second decisions about you based solely on a look in your eyes. You know how powerful a look or a glance can be in romance and personal relationships. Love at first sight is real. It may not be true love. That takes a little more time to cultivate, but sparks do fly at first sight. Same is true with selling and business relationships. As I've said before, relationships are relationships.

I'll never forget a conference I attended many years ago for meeting planners. I was a speaker at the event. I almost never hang around too much before or after I speak, but this time I did. I attended a seminar that was teaching meeting planners how to deal with hotel salespeople and get the best possible prices from them. I was so intrigued I took notes. The seminar leader listed 10 secrets to getting the best deal. I will reveal more in Chapter 7, but the very first thing on the list was to focus on the salesperson's eyes! I couldn't believe what I was hearing.

For years, I had taught salespeople that their eyes were the most important selling tool they own, but I never imagined a buyer's being taught to notice them first. The seminar leader went on to say that buyers can immediately discern how far to push and prod salespeople for a better price based solely on the look in their eyes. The seminar leader went on to say that the eyes also displayed whether or not salespeople could be trusted and counted on. If their eyes showed conviction and depth, then they could be counted on. If the salespeople avoided direct eye contact or made nervous, unsure, or erratic eye contact, then the buyer should not enter into any kind of business relationship with them. This was an eye-opening moment for me. Excuse the pun. It confirmed just how critical our eyes are in building relationships.

Now, I am not suggesting that every person you might deal with has been taught to focus on your eyes as a litmus test to working with you. What I am suggesting is that a person doesn't need to be taught this to form impressions and make snap judgments. I remember the exact moment I fell in love with my wife. We had just taken a jog around the block, and I was rubbing her shoulders as we watched TV back at my apartment and she leaned back and looked up at me as if to say thanks. Our eyes connected in a way that I had never experienced before. It was that moment that I thought to myself, she could be the one.

No one had to teach me the importance of a look in someone's eye. I didn't need an academic explanation. I knew what I felt. Selling moments may not be quite that dramatic, but those kinds of moments happen all the time. Neither party may realize it, but it's part of the visual dynamic of presence that just may be the spark that begins a relationship. Make sure you cultivate your love for what you sell, and be committed to service so that your eyes can rightly display your conviction to your customers.

Purpose

The second visual element of presence is *purpose*. Do not confuse purpose with reason. You have a reason to make a sales call. You want to make a sale. You may even have a scheduled appointment. The reason is obvious, and your potential customer understands this. All salespeople have a reason to sell, but very few have a purpose. The quick test to see if you have a purpose is if you can complete the following sentence: "If I could do anything in the world and make money doing it, it would be_____." Whatever you answer is the key to finding your purpose. Hopefully it has something to do with what you're selling.

I have often told salespeople to never make a single sales call again for the rest of their life. Sales managers everywhere cringe when they hear me say that, but it's sound advice. Who wants to make a sales call? That sounds like work, and no one likes to work. Instead, I tell sales reps to embark on a sales crusade! A crusade is a mission. It's a purpose. It says you believe in what you're doing with ever fiber of your being. If you can combine solid selling skills, genuine enthusiasm, and the belief that you are doing exactly what you were put on the earth to do, you will be absolutely irresistible and contagious.

There's a famous story many of us speakers have often told about having purpose. I am not sure where it originated but it's a good one:

One day a man came across three stone-cutters working in a quarry. Each one was cutting out a block of stone. Curious as to what they were doing, he asked the first stonecutter what he was doing. "What? Are you blind?" the stonecutter shouted. "Can't you see? I'm cutting this stupid piece of stone." Shocked but still no wiser, the man turned to the second stonecut-ter and asked him what he was doing. "I am cutting this block of stone to make sure that the sides are straight and smooth so the builder can build a straight wall." Feeling a lot better but still not sure what either of them was really doing, he turned to the third stonecutter, who seemed to be the happiest of the three, and asked him what he was doing. The third stonecutter replied, "I am building a cathedral."

The moral of the story is obvious. The first stonecutter was just doing his job. He didn't like his job, and the only reason he was doing it was for the paycheck. Many struggling sales-people fall into this category. It's not a calling; it's just a job. For salespeople in this category, turnover is high, career satisfaction is low, and achievement is inconsistent at best.

The second stonecutter took pride in his job. He had received certain instructions from his supervisor, and he was diligently following along. The majority of salespeople fall into this category. They like their job, and the like the kudos and recognition that come with a job well done, especially the money.

The third stonecutter had a purpose. He knew what he was doing and why he was doing it. He still enjoyed the money and the kudos, but the job wasn't about only those things. It was about helping people and doing something he could ultimately be proud of. Very few salespeople fall into this category, but those who do are the superachievers.

My own journey took me through all three. My first sales job was selling air filters. I wanted the job because I liked selling and thought I'd be pretty good at it, but it was just a job. It paid for my first apartment away from Mom and Dad. However, it wasn't just a job to the owner of the business. He fired me because he knew my heart wasn't in it. My second job was selling yellow pages. Determined to learn from my mistakes, I set goals and attacked the job with passion. I quickly moved up the ranks to a position of authority. I enjoyed the job and the success, but I hardly could say it was my life's mission.

My third job was selling sales training presentations that I conducted. For the first time, I felt like I had true purpose. I loved it—and I still do to this day—but that didn't mean it was always smooth sailing. There were many hard times that tested my resolve to this purpose. There were times when I wanted to call it quits. I recall one such period in my journey when I was rolling around in bed, unable to fall asleep, contemplating if I should just quit and try to find something else to do. Something more stable.

Maybe I should get a "real job," as my mother would say. Then something I remembered from my wedding vows hit me like a ton of bricks. I got married for better or worse, for richer or poorer. No one said it would be easy. In fact, anything and everything truly wonderful is NEVER easy. It was that night that I gave up stalking fame and fortune and focused on making a difference in people's lives. I know it sounds corny, but I was in it for better or worse, richer or poorer. That night it became my purpose, and my business took off. I still had some rough times, and there still times when I second-guessed myself, but they were fewer and further between. Purpose is a game changer in every profession, but in the world of selling, it's the difference between good and great!

Humility

The third element of presence is *humility*. On the surface, having both self-assuredness and humility may seem contradictory, and if either one is not genuine, it is. However, having true confidence means also being able and willing to exhibit your humble side. The key aha truth is that when you are humble, you are proportionately confident. When you are weak, you are proportionately strong. It takes a very self-assured person to show any level of vulnerability. Relationships are real. They aren't perfect. One of the biggest myths in selling is that there is absolutely no room for error. Not only is there room for error but it is inevitable. There may be perfect, error-free transactions, but there's no such thing as an error-free ongoing relationship. It's how you handle the errors and the things that go wrong that show your customers who you really are.

Customers want the same things in business relationships that people want in personal relationships. They want honesty, authenticity, integrity, and commitment. They want a partnership. To that end, the following three simple power statements are prime ways to exhibit humility and build stronger partnerships.

"I Don't Know"

People may get irritated if you don't have an immediate answer to something they may need, but it won't damage the relationship. What will, however, damage the relationship is if you fake your way through an answer or say something that is ultimately proven to be incorrect. There is no breach in honesty to admit you don't know something, but when you say something false or something that *may* be false, there is a major breach in honesty. So if something does go wrong, admit it right away.

There's an old adage in public relations that says when you admit a negative, the marketplace responds with a positive. But if you refuse to admit any wrongdoing, the marketplace doubles down on the negative. How many times do we see politicians fumble through explaining, justifying, and covering up mistakes when we know that things would ultimately go better for them if instead they just came out and admitted the mistakes? It's simply a matter of integrity.

Along the same lines is doing or not doing what you say. If you say you will call someone back in 5 minutes, make sure it is really

5 minutes. Calling someone back in 15 minutes instead of 5 may seem innocent and miniscule, but if the person can't count on your words, he or she can't (and won't) count on you. I'll have more to say about keeping your word in Chapter 8.

"You May Be Right"

This is the ultimate problem diffuser. Getting into debates with customers over who is right or wrong is almost always a no-win situation for any salesperson. If you prove your customers to be wrong, you feel good but they feel bad. If your customers prove you to be wrong, they feel good but you feel bad.

The win-win is to simply say, "You may be right." You're not saying they are right or wrong. You're saying only that there is a possibility. Unless the debate is over something ethical or potentially criminal, choose the high road and preserve the relationship. After all, "you never know!"—which is another one of my all-time favorite sayings!

"What Do You Think?"

Not only is this question a display of humility but it's also an empowering question as well. It's a question that invites inclusion. It shows that you not only value their opinion but also that you want their opinion. Salespeople often say that they value what their customers have to say. The problem is that they never ask for it. Relationships are based on give-and-take. They are unions of personalities, ideas, and mutually beneficial arrangements. At every chance you get, ask other people what they think. You'll be surprised at what you learn and how much it advances your relationships.

～

Bottom line: It's hard to discern how much of all this is real science and how much is just plain common sense. Being contagious does require adhering to some absolute dos and don'ts, but it's more about the intangibles than the tangibles. In the end, it's a little less science and little more romance.

CHAPTER 5

It's Not What You Say or Do; It's Who You Are

We're now at the point of the relationship when we've gotten face-to-face with a potential customer. In this chapter, we will explore the dynamics of the face-to-face sales appointment and identify the things that build contagiousness and keep the relationship moving forward.

THE PERSONAL QUALITIES THAT MAKE SALESPEOPLE SUCCESSFUL

I've been speaking and training sales reps for over 25 years, and I've had the privilege of standing in front of over a million people. The most-asked question of my career has been to identify the most important quality a salesperson can possess. Right off the top, I can name dozens including passion, motivation, persistence, organization, charm, and eloquence. However, if I had to name just one, it would overwhelmingly be curiosity.

Genuine curiosity is by far the most contagious quality a salesperson can exhibit. It's not something you say or do. It's who you are. It's a quality that needs to come from within. Being curious shows that you are more focused on other people than you are on yourself. It shows that you want to understand their needs and the challenges they face. It shows that you want to connect with them on a deeper level. It shows that you care.

HOW TO CULTIVATE YOUR CURIOSITY

So the next question is this: How can salespeople become curious or more curious than they already are? For starters, I believe everyone is naturally curious. Of course, some are more so than others, but every human being has the built-in trait of curiosity. There are many factors, including upbringing, that affect how curious people are, and there is data to suggest that we grow less curious as we get older. Curiosity is a quality that must continually be cultivated or we tend to gradually lose it until it's hardly there. It's a "use-it-or-lose-it" kind of thing. Since it is so important to selling and being contagious, I've dedicated this entire chapter to how we can become more curious. Although there are many ways to choose from, I believe the four simplest ways to cultivate your curiosity are these: zero in on your customer, ask questions, be a good listener, and be fascinated.

Zero in on Your Customer

The art of "zeroing in," as I like to call it, is easy to understand but very hard to execute. There are countless things that prevent us from zeroing in and instead getting sidetracked while on a sales call. If I had a nickel for every time a sales appointment has been interrupted by a phone call, a person popping in, or some other kind of unexpected intrusion, I'd be a very wealthy man. As the saying goes, "It happens." Added to this is the fact that most salespeople unwittingly create their own distractions in the name of rapport building. Let me explain.

For years, in almost every sales training seminar across America, sales trainers have been teaching salespeople to walk into a prospect's office and begin taking notice of things in the environment and décor in an effort to instantly build rapport. We've been taught to notice the prospects' Chicago Cubs banner and with laser beam speed say, "I see you're a Cubs fan. Could this finally be the year?" Perhaps we saw their diploma from the University of Southern California, and we were taught to ask, "I see you're from California. What brought you to the East Coast?"

This shallow act of show-and-tell seems harmless, and it actually started out to be very effective. But over the years, as more and more salespeople employed this tactic, it not only lost its effectiveness but it can hurt more than help. Buyers have caught on, and they recognize it as a sales tactic. Any sales tactics that are recognized by buyers as sales tactics are no longer effective. This tactic now is similar in its effect to a cheesy pick-up line in a personal relationship. If the other person thinks the interest is less than sincere, it will never work. Selling is no different.

As I've mentioned (and will get to in Chapter 7), I've even attended seminars for buyers in which they were taught to recognize certain sales tactics and to counteract them. One countersales measure is to never invite a salesperson into your personal office space. Buyers are taught that if they must meet with salespeople face-to-face, they should meet with them in a lobby or a conference room because these are neutral environments. Buyers are taught to eliminate the temptation for sales-people to ask them about their personal prefer-ences. If you've been in sales for any length of time, I'm willing to bet that you can recall off the top of your head instances in which you've had to conduct a sales presentation in a con-ference room. This is not to suggest that those have all been examples of buyers who had been formally taught to do that. However, it might be the case, and it does suggest that at the very least, your prospects don't want you in their office, for whatever reason.

So my remedy is to zero in on *them*, not their surroundings. By taking this approach, no one can ever accuse you of using some worn-out sales ploy. Plus, I believe it's a lot more effec-tive. Get right down to business. Stay on mes-sage. Just after shaking hands and being seated for the appointment, zero in and say, "I am so excited to have the opportunity to chat with you today. I am convinced that my company [or product or service] can be a tremendous asset to you. But before I get into just how, I'd like to learn a little more about your business." This opening statement does two things.

First, it builds excitement and anticipation for what you might have to say. You should be eager to talk about what you're there for. Talking about baseball or the weather or anything other than why you're there is just a distraction. If the customer brings up these things, it's perfectly OK to address them. I am not suggesting you be rigid and unwilling to be personal. I am only suggesting to let your customer get personal, not you. Forcing personal dialogue does more to hurt rapport than it does to help it. Instead, you want to stay on message and let them know that you couldn't wait for the opportunity to present your services. This kind of curiosity building statement must be genuine, and I suggest it be the first words, after a few greeting pleasantries, out of your mouth. You want the prospect to see the enthusiasm in your eyes, hear it in your voice, and feel it in your energy.

The second thing this statement does is take charge. On every single sales appointment, someone takes charge. I want it to be you. If your prospects detect that you don't have a plan, they will take charge. They will say things like "So tell me what you've got" or "I have only a few minutes so let's make this quick." These are telltale signs that they intend to take charge. By taking charge from the outset, you can generally avoid comments such as these. However, if you do still get them, simply restate the need to get a little more information from them first. Successful sales calls have an order. Don't let the prospects get you off message and out of order.

Ask Questions

The second way to cultivate curiosity is by asking questions. This may seem to be fairly obvious and elementary, but I am not talking about asking questions just to ask questions. Nor I am talking about asking just any kind of questions. I'm talking about the kind of questions that make your prospects think. This is probably the biggest opportunity that most salespeople miss. Every salesperson asks questions, but are they the right questions? Are they asked with a certain goal in mind other than just to gather superficial data? And what should you do while asking those questions?

There are two primary goals in asking questions: (1) to enable customers to see the ways in which you are different from other salespeople and (2) to gather information.

Ask Questions to Differentiate You from Other Salespeople

As to the first goal, you want to ask questions that differentiate you from every other salesperson that your prospects have met. You want to make them think.

I'll never forget a sales call I made with a salesperson with a staffing company. She asked a few questions and even scribbled a few notes. About three minutes into this, the customer stopped her in midsentence and said, "Does every staffing salesperson attend the same sales training class? Because all of you ask identical questions."

I tried to contain my smirk, but I knew that answer. The answer was yes!

Unfortunately a lot of salespeople, not just in the staffing industry, are trained to ask questions focused around the transaction. They ask a lot of logistical questions centered on gaining the necessary information to make a sale in the short term. Instead, we should be asking questions that make the prospects think and position us as a strategic partner. Our focus should be on getting an account for the long term. I've always said that average salespeople set out to make a sale; great salespeople set out to make a friend.

The kinds of questions I suggest are strategical, not logistical. I suggest open-ended questions instead of closed-ended questions. Open-ended questions cannot be answered with a yes or no. They usually begin with who, what, where, and why. A few suggestions might be to ask about how the prospects got to where they are, what their background is, what separates their company from their competition, what does their competition do right, what makes their company a good place to work, what are their plans for growth, what activities and/or products bring them the highest returns on investment, what are their biggest challenges, and what things top their wish lists. Depending on what you sell, these may need to be altered a bit, but you get the idea.

I want your prospects to say things like "That's a good question. No one has ever asked me that before." Or even "Why do you need to know that?" This gives you the opportunity to respond by saying, "I'm not interested in just making a one-time sale. I want to fully understand you, your company, and your needs to be able to do business with you for the next 20 years!"

A lot can be discovered by the type of questions you ask. Even if your prospects act irritated at your questions, deep down they will appreciate your curiosity at wanting to learn more about them. The only time you might want to ask a closed-ended question is when you've identified the customer as having either a fast rate/low inflection (FRLI) or a slow rate/low inflection (SRLI) speaking style and personality. Closed-ended questions usually begin with verbs such as *can*, *do*, *shall*, and *will*. Identifying the customers' vocal patterns and matching your questions to their communication style can pay huge dividends!

Ask Questions to Gather Information

The second goal of asking questions is of course to gather information. What has always amazed me when I've asked salespeople what they do with their gathered information is that many are not quite sure. It's as if they know they need to ask questions to get information, but they not sure as to how to use it. Some say they ask questions to show the customers they care. It's certainly true that many customers will respond that way, and we'll talk about that later in this chapter. Other salespeople say they just want to learn about their customers. These questions will also help them do that.

But there is yet another reason to gather information, and that's to use that information later. That is why it is absolutely imperative that you always take notes when asking questions. Taking notes sends the message to customers that what they are saying is important and that you want to remember what they say, which is exactly what you want to do anyway. You want to have a written record of their words so that long after the meeting, you can refresh your memory by reading your notes.

However, the second purpose of question asking is to uncover something that will help you close the sale. If you listen carefully and take good notes, all customers tell you exactly what you need to know to sell them. Not only do they reveal what they might and might not be looking for in salespeople but they are also very likely to give you information that will be valuable later. For example, I like to ask customers how much it costs to hire and train a new salesperson. Often the customer doesn't understand why I might want that information, but I'll use it later in my presentation to support my point that companies invest heavily in a new sales rep only to spend nowhere near that amount as they progress through their careers. This is but one example of stealth question asking to support a point you intend to make later.

Be a Good Listener

The third way to cultivate curiosity is be a good listener. This one seems obvious, but what isn't so obvious is that the crucial part of listening is that the other person believes you are listening. In other words, you are infinitely better off in the rapport department to not listen but have your customers think you are than to be actually listening but have your customers think you're not! Of course, it's best to do both, but I am amazed at how often salespeople sabotage their own listening by inadvertently sending messages that they aren't really listening. There are 10 natural listening obstacles that send the message that you really aren't listening even if you actually are. I realize that there may be many more, but these are the common offenders.

The listening obstacles are these:

1. ***Daydreaming*:** Who isn't and hasn't been guilty of daydreaming? Of course, the answer is no one! Daydreaming is a symptom of a lack of focus. It may be because you have trouble focusing or that you simply don't care. We all have trouble focusing at times. I know I probably have the adult form of ADHD, but even without that convenient excuse, my mind wanders all the time. The few days leading up to a vacation or holiday break is an especially bad time because we start picturing ourselves on a beach somewhere or sipping hot chocolate by the fireplace. Either way, we need to focus on our customers. We never want to have

to say, "I'm sorry, could you repeat that last thing you said? I was daydreaming!"

2. *Physical distraction*: This is when we are distracted by something physical. It could be something in the customers' office, on their wall, the outfit they're wearing, or they themselves. I remember one such time when I was completely distracted by a customer's eyeglasses. I remember thinking that I had never seen a thicker set of lenses in my life! They must have been an inch thick. I know I've also been distracted by ties, watches, and shoes. Not only is physical distraction obvious to your customers but it also makes them self-conscious, which becomes a barrier to rapport. They immediately make a rushed judgment about you that more than likely isn't true. All because you might have been admiring their shoes!

3. *Evaluating the dialogue*: This is when you evaluate the previous dialogue. You might be thinking about how you're doing, why they might have said what they said, or perhaps just replaying something in your mind. In any event, it's not a good thing to do. You miss what they're currently saying by evaluating a past statement. Stay focused on what

they're saying, not on what's already been said. There's plenty of time for evaluation and analysis later.

4. *Strategizing*: This is the future form of evaluating. This is strategizing as to what to say next. While you are mentally crafting your next words, you are not listening, and you may be missing something valuable.

5. *Speeding things up*: This one sneaks up on you. You might be in a rush and have less time for the appointment than is ideal, so subconsciously your thoughts go into hypergear. When I am guilty of this, I begin to nod my head excessively as if to attempt to speed things along. I think I am simply expressing agreement, but I am actually sending that "hurry up" message to my customer. Remember, unless your customer *thinks* you are listening, it doesn't matter if you actually are!

6. *Silent debate*: This is when we debate in our mind something that was said in the conversation. We immediately begin breaking it down and forming our rebuttal. Too often we seek to be right instead of seeking to understand. We often win the battle but lose the war.

Most salespeople are quick to debate,
both verbally and nonverbally, and
many times this is a relationship killer.
Again, a good litmus test is to contrast
selling with romance. How would you
feel if upon first meeting someone, that
person seemed to disagree with, debate,
and attack things you said? Chances
are, you'd feel less than enchanted.
The same is true in a selling situation.
Unless someone has said something
against your character, let it go. Try
to understand what he or she might
be trying to say instead of debating in
your mind.

7. *Selectiveness*: You can guess this one.
   It's hearing only what you want to hear.
   When my kids were little, they were
   masters at selective listening. I would
   say, "You can have a cookie after dinner,"
   but somehow the after-dinner part was
   never heard. They would swear that I
   had never said it, and I'm sure that was
   their recollection. They heard what they
   wanted to hear and then tuned out and
   moved on. This happens in selling all the
   time. We know what we are hoping to
   hear so when we get it, we immediately
   jump to pass go!

8. ***Jumping to conclusions***: This one almost always accompanies another obstacle. For instance, because we engage in silent debate, we then jump to conclusions. Because we are in a hurry, we jump to conclusions, or as soon as we hear what we want, we jump to conclusions. As with all the obstacles, you may miss something really important and send nonlistening signals when you jump to conclusions. Not to mention that your conclusion may be wrong!

9. ***Antagonism***: This is where your personal feelings become the actual obstacle. There have been a few rare occasions when I just simply did not care for my customers personally. Maybe it was because of something they did or said, or maybe it was just because our personalities clashed. I immediately got defensive, and this became a barrier to listening and even the relationship. Whatever the reason, antagonism isn't healthy. So if you can rise above your initial feelings, a working relationship is still a possibility. My wife's very first words to me were "Get lost!" Granted, they were in response to a very cheesy line on my part, but her first reaction was

antagonistic. Thankfully, she didn't shut down to me, and when I approached her again with more genuine dialogue, she was receptive and a relationship ensued. Many times, business relationships also get off to a rocky start. It isn't the end. Just regroup and chalk it up to someone's having a bad day. There truly are such things as second, and third, chances in relationships!

10. *False courtesy*: This happens when we become preoccupied with sending the message that we're listening but it has the opposite effect. Anything that is not of true genuineness is not genuine. If something is only 5 percent fake, it's 100 percent not genuine. If you listen only 99 percent of the time, the 1 percent you don't listen is enough for you to compromise the relationship. Courtesy that is not real will always be exposed.

As stated, the preceding list is not the definitive list of listening obstacles, but it's enough to get the picture. Listening is not an exercise in hearing; it is an act of caring. In fact, you listen as much with your eyes as you do with your ears. Ears catch the words, but your eyes show your interest. You have to want to be a good listener to actually be one. It's dynamic and on purpose, but there's no better way to cultivate curiosity than to ask good questions and be a good listener.

Be Fascinated

The fourth and final way of cultivating curiosity is through sheer fascination. You need to have childlike amazement and wonder. I can still remember how excited I got as an eight-year-old when my mom came home with a chocolate lollipop from Howard Johnson's and how excited my own kids got when it first began to snow. I remember as if it were yesterday how big my son's eyes got when he first saw the playground at Universal Studios. Those were magical times and ones I'll never forget. But what happened? Somehow as we get older, we lose the magic. We lose the childlike amazement and wonder. We lose the ability to be supercurious. But the good news is that we can get it back. It's not so much that it's lost than that it is buried under the heap of experience and disappointment. However, rekindling the fascination for discovering new things is one of the prime secrets to connecting with other human beings!

Start with the fascination for the company whose doors you just walked into. Think like an eight-year-old. Eight-year-olds have no trouble asking "Why?" They are simply naturally curious. Ask yourself, and better yet, ask your customers "Why?" Take stock as to what their office or building entrance looks like. Why did they choose that location? How did they come up with their logo? Why do people work there? How did they get started in the business? Ask about the products and/or services they sell. How do they work? How are they built? Why do their customers like them? Be fascinated.

It's important to note the dual effect being fascinated has. First, it can gain you insights and answers you may never have gotten by merely conducting a "needs analysis." There's no fascination with a needs analysis. There's no magic. Every halfway decent salesperson conducts one. Fascination can separate you from the pack. Customers will tell you things they would never reveal in a traditional Q&A exchange. Sure you should ask questions. I covered the questions part earlier in this chapter, but now I want to cover the asking part. What you ask and how you ask are the magic. Ask with amazement and wonder. Ask for a demonstration. Ask for a tour of the building and operation. Ask for a sample. Ask to meet their team. Ask like an eight–year-old. Ask with fascination. Just ask!

Being fascinated is also extremely contagious. If there is such a thing as a universal truth, it is this: people's favorite subject is themselves! When you show genuine fascination and interest in your customers, they will respond favorably. This is why it must be genuine. People can spot a fake from a mile away, and once they perceive you as less than sincere, your fascination will be manipulative instead of contagious. However, as a salesperson, you should genuinely be interested in your customers. This shouldn't be such a leap. Start by resisting the temptation to do too much talking. The rule of thumb is that on any sales call, you should talk 25 percent of the time or less and listen 75 percent of the time or more. By keeping to this rule, you will ensure that the center of attention is exactly where it needs to be: on them! Not only will they consciously like the interest that you are showing but they will subconsciously catch your energy as well. Everyone has a little kid inside him or her who is dying to come out. People may not match your childlike fascination, but rest assured they want to. True fascination, like contagiousness, is something you possess. It is not something you say or do.

CHAPTER 6

Making a Contagious Presentation

While there are no universal sales presentations, the one thing that is certain is that a presentation is a vital part of the sales process. It's your chance to captivate your customers. There are a few unique aspects of the sales presentation in comparison to other sales situations. The first is that it is the *only* time in the sales process that is a monologue. Your presentation should be the time for you to explain to your customers why they should do business with you. It is your time to shine. I have found that the exact extent to which salespeople were good listeners during their fact-finding is the extent to which their customers listen during the sales presentation. If you've allowed your customers ample time to talk while you listened intently, they will return the courtesy. If not, expect interruptions and short attention spans.

THE ELEVATOR PITCH

There are two types of presentations that we will be exploring in this chapter: the elevator pitch and the formal presentation. The *elevator pitch*, or what I call the *pitch*, is just that. It is not a full-fledged presentation but rather a 10-second advertisement for what you do. It got the "elevator" name in reference to the fact that people should be able to fully explain to other people what they do in the time it takes for an elevator to travel between floors.

The goal of the pitch is not only to have people fully understand what you do but also to entice them to want to know more. For instance, my pitch is this: "I teach individuals and companies how to be contagious through customized speaking programs, marketing consulting, and trade published books." Their next response is almost always one of being intrigued and wanting more specifics. Most want to know what I mean by the word *contagious*, but whatever it was that sparked their curiosity, it accomplished what it was intended to do.

In light of how many networking functions and opportunities salespeople have every day, it has always surprised me how many salespeople don't have a prepared pitch. They either can't fully explain what they do within the required 10 seconds, or they say something generic and boring like "I sell office supplies." This may be concise and to the point, but it dead ends. It neither lights any sparks nor needs further explanation. Good salespeople are selling all the time, not just when they sitting in front of a prospect on an official sales call. Your pitch is an opportunity to advertise what you do and sell yourself. People buy you before they ever buy whatever you might be selling. This is a golden opportunity to display your passion and be contagious. Make it count.

THE FORMAL PRESENTATION

The formal, traditional sales presentation is for those times when you are on a sales call and must educate your customers on your product or service. But, as with everything in relationships, timing and order are crucial. A presentation must never be made out of order. It should always be made AFTER sufficient fact-finding, and never before.

The order of a successful sales call is as follows: **preparation, approach, fact-finding, presentation, recommendation, and close.**

Any variation in that order will upset the apple cart and handicap your chances of a sale. Your customers may try to save time and ask you to cut to the chase, but don't take the bait. I've had customers tell me point blank just after shaking their hand that they only have a few minutes and want me to go straight to the price. They mean well, and I am sure they are sincere in wanting to save time, but you would be doing them a huge injustice if you did that. When this happens, you need to politely tell them that you will be as brief as possible but that for their sake you need to learn a little bit about them first. This is where you need to take charge and show some salesmanship. You know you want to build a relationship with them, but they don't know it yet. In romantic terms, you want to date them, but they may or may not feel the same way. You can't take shortcuts when trying to win them over.

Similarly, you can't take shortcuts to make a sale either. Never make your presentation until it's time. And you always want to make a *transition statement* when going from fact-finding into your presentation. A transition statement is necessary because you are shifting dynamics from a two-way conversation to one-way monologue. I suggest something like this: "Thank you for the information you provided. I really enjoyed learning about your organization. I'd now like to tell you a little about my company, if that's OK?" That is just an example.

You'll be using your own words, of course, but a transition statement does several things. First, it shows organization and that you have a plan. Customers appreciate that you're not just winging the sales call. The sales call is your first date. You want to show you've given this thought. If you wing the sales call, they might think you'll wing every facet of the relationship as well. Second, it postures you as being in charge. It instills confidence in you. It sends the message that you believe in what you're doing and that they should trust where you're going. If done right, and if you've been a good listener, they will welcome sitting back and extending you their undivided attention as you make your presentation.

NINE QUALITIES OF AN EFFECTIVE PRESENTATION

With that said, there are two, and only two, dynamics of what makes people buy that must be present in any presentation. People buy because they either want to gain an advantage or avoid a disadvantage. Some call it "hope to gain" and "fear of loss," or "gain or pain."

Either way, every buying decision can be put in one of those two categories, and of the two, fear of loss is a stronger motivator than hope to gain. People would like to succeed, but most aren't willing to go the extra mile to do so. However, no one wants to fail.

Avoiding failure is a stronger motivator than the desire to win. Ask any coach in any sport. In advertising circles, you see this at play all the time. "Quantities are limited," "only 10 left in stock," "while supplies last," and "for a limited time only" are prime examples of playing to the fear of loss. In selling, it's often referred to as *take-away selling*. Taking something away or telling people that they may not get something is a surefire way to get them to want it even more. So, by making sure your presentation contains both motivators (hope to gain and fear of loss), you will maximize the contagiousness level dramatically. We will explore how to do that specifically as we look at the nine qualities of an effective presentation.

1. It Is Well Organized

Make sure your presentation is organized and that everything has a point. I've had the privilege of being witness to thousands of sales presentations in my career, and I am continually amazed at how unorganized and random most of them are. Sales presentations seem to go to one of two extremes. Either the company mandates that their sales reps memorize and recite a well-scripted diatribe, or the company leaves it to the salespeople to craft their own message. I don't like either approach. I don't like a memorized presentation because it often doesn't leave any room for customization.

A good presentation incorporates the information just learned from fact-finding, and reciting a memorized script makes that hard to do. Conversely, a good presentation should not be winged. What I suggest is somewhere in between those two extremes. While I do want salespeople to have an organized, rehearsed, well-thought-out presentation, I also want them to have enough flexibility to use information on the fly that they may have just gotten.

Salespeople need to know and memorize an outline for their presentation so that they cannot be knocked off course, but they must remain flexible within that outline. I could be awakened at 3 o'clock in the morning from a deep slumber and give my presentation. It would be void of any custom information since I wouldn't have just conducted any fact-finding, but nonetheless, I could give one. And since I am not scripted to the word, each time I give a presentation, it is slightly different from the last. The main points are always there, and I follow the same outline, but I am free to be me and personalize my presentation with any new information I may have gotten.

Bottom line: Be organized, be prepared, and have an outline for every presentation. The words in between should be tailored to the customers.

2. It Moves from the General to the Specific

The second quality of an effective, and contagious, presentation is that it moves from the general to the specific. This is just good common sense. When you first meet people, you don't begin by telling them the most intimate details of your life. You begin with the basic big picture and get more specific as you go. Same is true with a good presentation.

A good presentation is a story. It has a set-up, a plot, and climax. I often even refer to presentations as "stories" because it helps salespeople think of it in the right way. Start by telling them about your company—how long it's been in business, how it got started, why it got started, where it's located, and similar logistical, general information. Then talk about your products and services, and gradually get more and more specific as you go.

Don't talk about things that have no relevance to your customers because doing so will only muddy the water by giving them too much unnecessary information. You want to gradually hone in on the exact product or service that you will be recommending for those customers. Giving too much information is a major mistake that many salespeople make. Don't take a scattered shotgun approach hoping that something you say will hit the target. Rather, use a snipe approach that takes direct aim at precisely what will most benefit the customers.

3. It Translates Features into Bottom-Line Benefits

An effective presentation always translates features into bottom-line benefits. Things like your company's state-of-the-art facilities, online ordering capabilities, or 24-hour customer service are not benefits. They are features. I know this may sound ridiculously elementary, but way too many sales presentations are chock-full of features that are never translated into benefits. A *feature* is prominent aspect, quality, or characteristic. A *benefit* is what that aspect, quality, or characteristic does for the customer.

A lesson I learned in my very first sales training class was to find the bottom-line benefit by always following a feature with the words "and what that means to you is." For instance, a salesperson might say, "We've got a 24-hour customer service hotline, and what that means to you is that whenever and wherever you want or need to call us, you can do it. And this saves you time by your not having to wait until Monday morning if you need us over the weekend." The bottom-line benefit here is saving time. Most benefits come down to saving time, saving money, having peace of mind, or making your customers look good, but never assume that your customers make the mental translation. By always following a feature in your presentation with a bottom-line benefit, you will be letting your customers know that everything you mention has the purpose of benefiting them.

4. It Focuses on Your Uniqueness

Focus on what you can do, not what the competition can't. Focus on your uniqueness and how you can help your customers. Way too common are the sales presentations that spend too much time and energy on the competition.

Contrary to what one might think, every time you mention your competition, you push your customers that much further from you! How would you feel if you were on a date with someone and he or she kept bringing up someone else? What would you think if your date kept talking about his or her ex? It doesn't matter whether he or she was saying good things or bad things. The mere fact that your date brought up his or her ex at all would be an unnecessary distraction at best and a complete turnoff at worst.

Customers want the salespeople that they do business with to be confident and able to stand on their own strengths, not on the weaknesses of others. You want someone to love you because of what you bring to the dance, not because you're the lesser of two evils. You may celebrate the commission, but if customers do business with you because your competition is inadequate, you are on shaky ground. It's only a matter of time before someone else makes you inadequate. Discover and exploit the things that you, and only you, can do.

One of the most important questions salespeople can answer is, "Why should someone buy from you?" In other words, "What makes you unique?" How they answer this question is often the difference between being average and being great. Great salespeople have a specific answer ready to go. Average salespeople hem and haw with generic, nonspecific answers.

5. It Respects That You Are Part of the Presentation

Always remember that YOU are part of the presentation. The message is never as important as the messenger. What you say is important, but how you say it and how you look are even more important. To repeat something I said before: people buy based on subjective experience, but they validate their decision with logic.

Trust and likability always trump data. Have you ever lost a sale to another company that you knew beyond a shadow of a doubt was inferior to yours? Of course you have. We all have. It means someone else had a stronger connection with the customer than you did. This is proof that emotion is stronger than information. To give the information that you have to present a fighting chance, you need to make sure that the delivery vehicle is solid is well. YOU are the delivery vehicle.

Be sure your voice pattern matches the customers'. We talked about this in Chapter 4. If during your two-way fact-finding conversation, you noticed that your customers were communicating in a slow rate/high inflection (SRHI) voice, you should then deliver your presentation in the same SRHI voice. Communicate with them the way they have been communicating with you. In fact, you should have four different presentations rehearsed and ready to go. And each one should be based on the four different vocal patterns. You never want to deliver a fast rate/high inflection (FRHI) presentation to people who are speaking in a slow rate/low inflection (SRLI) voice. You won't connect, and then you will wonder why they decided to do business with someone else.

Before customers buy your product or service, they must first buy YOU. Matching them vocally doesn't guarantee that you'll have an instant connection, but not matching them will guarantee you won't. It may be a small thing, but it's one that can make a huge, often subconscious, difference.

While I could spend an entire chapter on this one topic, there is one big mistake that many salespeople make that I must address, however briefly. They rely too heavily on technology or props. While both take the pressure off of you, they also take the spotlight off of you. Both appeal to logic at the expense of emotion.

A supporting chart, illustration, or photo is good, but don't go overboard in the midst of a presentation. You can leave those things behind as supporting data, but your presentation is your one shot to truly connect. Don't give up your spotlight. And don't forget that technology can fail.

I've personally witnessed dozens of well-crafted PowerPoint presentations go south because something wouldn't work properly. Fiddling around trying to get something to work not only wastes valuable time but it also creates unspoken awkwardness that is hard to overcome.

The overuse of technology also takes your customers' eyes off of you. I mean literally as well as figuratively. Connection is made through the eyes! The more solid the eye contact, the deeper the rapport. Of course, eye contact can also be abused. You shouldn't stare as if to try to wear down or intimidate your customers. Nor should you look down or past your customers when talking to them. This will only make them wonder what you're looking at. Focus on them, and they will focus on you. You want your eyes to communicate trust and believability. They are the window to your soul and the heart of any contagious presentation.

6. It Invites Feedback

Make sure you get a little feedback during your presentation. Since your presentation is essentially a monologue, the last thing you want is to get to the end of your presentation only to find that you lost your customers at some point without ever realizing it. To make sure this doesn't happen, you'll want to pepper your presentation with a few questions such as these: "How does that sound?" "Does this sound like something you can use?" "Can you see how this will save you a great deal of time?"

Feel free to customize the questions for your presentations. These are also trial closes. By getting your customers to agree to several smaller decisions throughout the presentation, you enhance your odds of doing business with them. These small victories add up. It's a similar dynamic to having a great time on a first date. If a lot of little things go well throughout the evening, the odds go up that you'll land a second date. If there weren't a lot of things the two of you agreed on, your odds of a second date aren't very good. This quality is where the selling axiom Always Be Closing (ABC) gets its name. You get the ultimate yes by getting a series of smaller yeses throughout the presentation.

7. It Does Not Oversell

Avoid redundancies, and do not oversell. Overselling is much more rampant than most salespeople would care to admit, but that's largely because most salespeople don't realize they're doing it. Overselling occurs (a) when the customers are ready to buy but the salesperson has failed to recognize it and continues to talk or (b) when the salesperson continues to mention every feature and benefit regardless of its relevance to the customers. Either scenario can be fatal because it can lead to actually talking customers out of a sale!

The very best way to avoid overselling is by not shortchanging the fact-finding process. Overselling occurs more frequently when salespeople have either abbreviated their fact-finding or skipped it altogether. By not having the benefit of the information learned in fact-finding, salespeople feel the need to talk about everything in the hopes of hitting on something of interest to the customers. This shotgun approach to presenting has killed more sales than a hunter during deer season. Overselling also can occur when salespeople are oblivious to any buying signals the customers give. Buying signals include a big smile or excessive nodding in approval or agreement; taking possession of your product after your presentation; asking about color, delivery, or warranty; or reaching for and holding a pen.

Whenever you spot a buying signal, react immediately. Go straight to pass go regardless of where you might be in your presentation. Continuing past a buying signal for any amount of time is overselling and can jeopardize the sale. Same too with overselling by information overload. An effective presentation should be 6 to 12 minutes. No more, no less. Any longer is usually overselling, and any shorter is usually insufficient. While there may be some industries that require a longer, more detailed and theatrical presentation, the overwhelming majority do not. Practice giving your presentation to make sure you fall within the 6 to 12 minutes. Your presentation is your big moment. It's your time in the batters' box. Be ready to hit it out of the ballpark. Every time!

8. It Assumes the Sale

You never want to act surprised when customers say yes. Nor do you want to have to fumble for a contract or the necessary documents to complete a sale. Either action shows that you weren't prepared by not expecting a positive outcome.

Assuming the sale not only demonstrates confidence but it also can close sales that otherwise might not have been ready to close. I read somewhere many years ago that the average person makes two major decisions a year. Most decisions are minor ones such as where to go to lunch, what movie to rent, or whether to have chocolate or vanilla. The human tendency is to avoid making decisions until absolutely necessary. So when you come along asking for a decision, most people choose to kick the can down the road as long as they can.

Assume they will buy, and always be ready. I advocate going as far as having your paperwork filled out ahead of time as much and as often as possible. Sure, there are times when it's nothing more than wasted paper, but it's a gamble worth taking. Some customers who are on the fence will just go with it when they see that you believe so deeply in what you're selling. Confidence is contagious, and assuming the sale can be the tipping point some customers need. Average salespeople hope to sell and get excited when they make a sale. Great salespeople expect to sell and get disappointed when they don't.

9. It Dictates the Next Step

You want to dictate the next step, whatever that might be. Usually the next step is to make a solid recommendation accompanied by your price if applicable. Salespeople in some industries aren't able to talk about price even at this stage because they need more research and thought. If you can talk about price, be sure you wait until the end of your presentation. In fact, that moment should be the very first time that price gets talked about if at all.

Regardless of whether price gets talked about, all presentations should end with a recommendation from the salesperson. That recommendation might be to flat out ask for the business. It might be to set up another appointment or to go back to the drawing board for some more ideas. Whatever it might be, it needs to come from you.

You never want dead air after a presentation. Nor do you want to end a presentation by saying, "Well, what do you think?" This is like ending a date by asking, "Do you like me?" That shows a supreme lack of confidence, and it is a real momentum killer. Take charge and keep the relationship moving forward by dictating a next step. I often use those very words. I want my customers to know I have a plan, and most of the time, they appreciate that.

After every sales presentation there is an opportunity to advance the relationship. I also know that if I don't dictate a next step, the customer will. Someone will take charge. It should always be you. You want it to keep moving forward even if it is ever so slightly. If it's not moving forward, it's either stalled or dead, and neither is an acceptable place to be.

$\sim$

Selling is a dance. You want to be in charge, but you don't want to step on your customers' toes. You want a dip and kiss at the end, but you don't want to get slapped. You want to focus on them to make sure you don't miss any cues that might tell you what they are thinking.

You want to gaze into their eyes, but not so long and hard that they feel uncomfortable. You want to be eloquent, but you don't want to be so slick that you don't seem sincere. And most of all, you want to see them again. You want a next step. After all, the dance is just the beginning.

CHAPTER 7

What's All the Fuss About Price?!

The presentation is over, and you've made a solid recommendation for a next step. Now what? We all know what to do if the next step was granted and all was agreed upon and no one had to talk about money at all. But that often isn't reality. Things can get sticky when you have to talk money. This chapter is dedicated to how to talk about price with a potential buyer.

I once had a salesperson tell me something after one of my seminars that almost floored me. He said that he genuinely loved his job and loved his company. The only thing he didn't like was when he had to talk about price. He went on to say that selling would be the ideal profession if price were never brought up and never an issue. After a brief moment of silence as I expected him to say he was just kidding, I naturally responded by telling him how foolish that comment was. That's like saying that romance would be easy if everyone were in love with you.

Of course, selling would be a lot easier if you never had to deal with price, payment, and budget objections, but then it wouldn't be selling. It would be order taking. Effectively dealing with money issues is what separates professional selling from order taking. That's not to say that salesmanship is not required in order taking, but effectively talking about price is a higher-level talent that only great salespeople master.

We are going to explore the responses that occur after your sales presentation and specifically how to master the subject of price. My goal is that at the end of the chapter, you too will say, "What's all the fuss about price?!"

THE FOUR WAYS CUSTOMERS RESPOND

There are four common responses after a presentation: *yes*, *no*, *maybe*, and *not now*. There are variations on each, but almost every response falls into one of those four. I won't spend much time on *yes*, and only a little bit more time on *no*. They are relatively easy. It's the *maybe* and *not now* that are a lot tougher to deal with.

Everyone wants a *yes*, and if you aren't sure what to do with a *yes* response, you probably ought to consider another profession. After getting any form of a positive response, shut up and start executing the agreement. If that involves paperwork, get going on that immediately without continuing to talk. Anything you say after they've agreed to buy from you, with the exception of thanking them, will not help you. It can only hurt you. To put it in romance perspective, it's like continuing to talk after the other person has already agreed to kiss you. The time for talking is over, and is now time for action.

Your customers could also say *no*. While I always like to understand their thinking behind that answer, there isn't much that can be done right then and there. Ask them how they've arrived at that decision and if there's any room for changing their decision in the future. Sometimes the door will remain cracked open, and sometimes you'll get valuable feedback to help you with future prospects, but I never suggest debating customer over their decisions. If you asked someone out for a date and he or she said *no*, would you argue or try to talk him or her out of that decision? Probably not, unless the way he or she said it implied there was some wiggle room. Any debating only solidifies the customers' decision and guarantees an unfavorable impression. It's best to learn what you can about their decision, accept responsibility that you didn't do a good enough job in selling them, and move on. Perhaps there was a circumstance beyond your control that was the reason for their decision.

I recall a time after I had thought I had made an excellent presentation and the customer gave me an emphatic *no*. He declined to elaborate, so I thanked him for his time and left. Two days later someone in his department called me and informed me of his departure from the company and invited me back in to meet. He had said *no* because he was in the midst of quitting.

These things happen, but regardless of the reason or circumstances, learn to pick yourself up, brush yourself off, and get on to the next prospect. Letting a negative experience affect you for more than five minutes will only handicap the next selling opportunity. There are plenty of books that focus on how to handle rejection so I won't belabor the point. Suffice it to say that rejection is a built-in part of any profession (or endeavor) where relationships are center stage. Remember the famous quote from Winston Churchill: "If the present tries to sit in judgment of the past, it will lose the future." In other words, if you dwell on your failures you won't be ready and able to capitalize on the next opportunity. Being rejected is at the heart of selling and romance. Accept it, learn from it, and move on. Not everyone will love you. It's just that simple.

Yes and *no* are easy compared to *maybe* and *not now*. *Yes* and *no* are black and white, while the others are solidly gray. *Maybe* and *not now* mean there are conditions. Most of the time those responses are negotiating tactics. The best way to understand a *maybe* response is, of course, to relate it to a personal romantic situation.

Let's say you asked someone out on a date and she said "Maybe" or "Not now." How would you interpret that? Well, you'd probably think one of two things. Either she had certain stipulations under which she would agree to the date, or she was holding out for a better offer. Either is better than a flat out rejection, but neither is ideal. It means that she was not fully convinced. In selling, it means you haven't sufficiently sold the customers. There's something holding them back, and its imperative you find out what it is.

The easiest and best way to do that is by asking. Most salespeople never ask. They accept a nondecision hook, line, and sinker. If customers don't have to make a decision, they usually won't, and many times customers use noncommittal as an easy way to get rid of you. They don't expect you to probe into the reasons behind their indecisiveness. What they expect you to do—because it's what most salespeople do—is pack up quickly and ask when to follow up.

Following up on a nondecision is just delaying the inevitable. You need more information, if for no other reason than to know where you might have gone wrong. I suggest saying something like this: "While I respect your undecidedness, I am disappointed in myself for not doing an adequate job of demonstrating how beneficial my product and services can be to you. If I may ask, what exactly is holding you back from making a decision to do business with me?" This may seem very direct and to the point, but that's why I like it. The honesty and bluntness usually catch the customers off guard to the point that they have no option but to be honest and blunt in return. Something is holding them back, and until you know what that is, there's no way the relationship can move forward.

As a matter of fact, any objection that arises after a sales presentation can be handled by the same direct response. Most objections are not really objections. We mistakenly see them as negative, but objections are a good thing. They are conditions. It means they are seriously considering your proposal; however, you must make sure you're dealing with the real objection or concern and not some fabricated negotiating tactic. You do this by asking questions such as the one we just discussed. You don't want to get into a verbal game of tennis. They lob out an objection; you answer. This is usually a big waste of time. When you get an objection, ask, "Is this the only concern that is holding you back from making a decision?" If they say *yes*, answer it. If they say *no*, it's usually best to find out all their concerns before you say another thing.

Which brings us to the elephant in the room, and that's dealing with price. Many times, a conditional response is a way to get you to cave in on price. Most objections are primers to get a better deal. Savvy buyers know how to stoke the fire to get the best price out of salespeople. I realize this seems like gamesmanship, but it's a necessary part of the relationship building process. It's a subconscious test to see if you believe in your price. They want to test your mettle.

It's a way to see if they can trust you. The link between how you talk about price and how much they trust you is huge. It's like talking about politics and religion in a personal relationship, but it must be done. It's the proverbial bridge to the next stage of the relationship. It may be gamesmanship, but it's a game you had better be good at.

An interesting thing has happened in the world of corporate education over the past 15 years. Up until that time, sales, marketing, and customer service topics were the undisputed leaders in popularity and frequency. While they remain popular, there have been other topics that have challenged their position on the totem pole.

An obvious one is technology. Technology has certainly increased as a corporate educational emphasis, but a topic that has flown under the radar is *institutional purchasing*. In other words, teaching buyers, or anyone who has buying responsibilities, how to deal with salespeople.

"TEN TIPS TO A BETTER PRICE"

I first noticed this at a conference for meeting planners in the late 1990s. The most popular breakout sessions were on the subjects of negotiating better prices and rates, and how to combat selling techniques. I almost never sit in on sessions at conferences where I am speaking, but one session captured my attention so much that I sat in and took notes. It was called "Ten Tips to a Better Price." Since I taught salespeople how to hold their ground and get better margins, I thought it would be fun to hear the other side.

Well, it was not only interesting, but it has transformed my own seminars. I started included the 10 tips I learned that day in my programs and how to counter them from the sales side of the ledger. Before we explore those 10 tips, it is imperative I share the presenter's opening sentiments. He prefaced his remarks by saying that there were two kinds of relationships. One was built on price, and the other was built on value. He said that relationships built on value are mutually prosperous and will be sustained of the participants' own volition. Those kinds of relationships need little training and guidance. He would focus on the relationships built on price.

This was eye-opening and jaw dropping. I knew this was true from a salesperson's perspective, but I had no idea that it was seen the same way on the other side. It reinforced everything I believed about building relationships, and it has become the impetus of this book. Real, long-term relationships must be built around mutual value and trust and not just because you have the best deal in town.

From a sales perspective, this makes the 10 tips I am about to share all the more critical to counter. If you can't move the relationship past the price issue and on to value, your standing with your customers is on very thin ice. It's like the person who agrees to go on a dinner date with you simply because there was nothing better to do, and after all, he needed to eat. It fills a need, but it doesn't build a relationship. It also doesn't mean it's a bad thing. Sometimes dates are dates and sales are sales, even if they don't lead to anything long term. However, it's important to recognize them for what they are and not to deceive yourself into thinking you have something you don't. Sales made because of prices are *transactional*, not *relational*. They are lost in the blink of an eye the next time another person beats your prices. You're always looking over your shoulder wondering who is lurking in the shadows. It's not a solid footing for anyone in sales.

Tip 1. Pay Attention to the Salesperson's Eyes

The first of the 10 tips deals with something I wrote about in an earlier chapter. When I first heard it, I thought it was a bit unusual because it was a page right out of one of my sales seminars. The first tip for buyers was to *pay attention to the salesperson's eyes*. That's right, the salesperson's eyes! As strange as that may sound, it makes a lot of sense. Eyes show a myriad attributes. They show passion, commitment, sincerity, and whether someone is telling the truth.

But the one thing in particular buyers are taught to look for in the eyes is to get a sense of how easy the salespeople will be able to negotiate with. They are taught to notice any uneasiness or hesitancy that might signal weakness. In Chapter 4, I wrote about the importance of our eyes, so I won't cover already trodden ground, but it bears repeating that regardless of what buyers have been formally taught to look for, this happens in every sale, in every relationship, all the time. It may not be an on-purpose, or even a conscious, calculation, but our eyes are either our greatest strength or our greatest weakness in every encounter. Our eyes are the center of our universe.

Tip 2. Create Multiple Buying Influences

The second tip buyers are taught is to create *multiple buying influences* (MBIs). In other words, buyers are taught to create escape hatches by letting salespeople know that they will have to check with other people or a committee before making a decision. Sometimes this is true, but most of the time it is simply a convenient way to say *no*, or at least to stall.

The mistake salespeople make is that they take the bait by asking how they can get in front of the other decision makers or committee. If there really are other people or a committee helping make the buying decision, by asking to meet them, you risk insulting the buyers you are presently dealing with, or at least damaging their ego, by suggesting that you need to get in front of the rest of the decision-making unit. If there really are no other people involved or no committee, nothing constructive is gained by calling the buyers' bluff.

So the only positive way to deal with MBIs, real or fabricated, is to ignore them. I don't mean to pretend you didn't hear them but rather to treat the MBIs as inconsequential to the relationship, which they are! Your job is to connect with the people you're already in front of. Don't worry about anyone else.

If there really are other decision makers, there are only two possible outcomes. The first is that you haven't fully sold the people you are in front of, and they will go to the others asking for their input. You haven't created allies, so they don't want to stick their neck out and go to bat for you. The other possible outcome is that you have so strongly convinced the people in front of you to make the purchase that they will go to the others with a mandate to do business with you. Obviously, you'd prefer the latter. The only way that is possible is by ignoring MBIs and focusing on the relationship at hand.

Tip 3. Avoid Meeting a Salesperson Face-to-Face Whenever Possible

They even have a name for the third tip: they call it the *art of avoidance*. Buyers are taught to conduct business by e-mail and fax and to solicit bids where decisions can be made void of any emotion and strictly by bottom-line price. More and more industries are using the bid process to select the people they do business with.

This is obviously the exact opposite of what you want to do. You are looking for a relationship. They are not. Have you ever had an experience in which you wanted to date someone but that person did not want to date you? You knew he'd like you if he only gave you the chance. You can't win people over if you can't get with them eyeball to eyeball. The same is true with buyers. You must give them some compelling reason to meet with you.

Sure, there are some situations in which you can woo prospects by e-mail until they relent, but more often than not, e-mails only give the prospects the information they need without meeting you, and the e-mails can work against you more than they work for you. So, whether customers ask you to do business by e-mail, fax, or sealed bid, your job is do something to catch their attention and capture their curiosity enough to want to meet you. There are many ways to do that, and I don't want to blunt your creativeness by giving you examples. It's got to come from the heart, and it's got to be uniquely you.

Buyers are also taught that if they must meet with salespeople, *they should meet them on neutral territory*. They are taught to meet in the lobby, someone else's office, or at the corner restaurant. The reason is along the same lines as the reason for not wanting to meet you in the first place. It's to avoid the personal element. If you ever met with prospects in one of these places and wondered why, now you know.

Buyers don't want you to have a glimpse into their personal lives by inviting you into their personal space, and this has been exasperated by the fact that every sales training class in the past 20 years has taught salespeople to do just that. Salespeople have been taught to walk into their customers' office and take inventory. If they've got a picture of their family, ask about it. If there's a sports team connection, ask about it. If there's a clue as to their favorite hobby, ask about it. It's a technique that is so abused and overused that today's buyers know what you're trying to do and they are taught to circumvent it. It is recognized as a sales technique and a shallow attempt to build rapport.

Any technique that is recognized as a sales technique has lost its effectiveness. It is seen only as manipulative and fake. So the way you counter this tip is by keeping things professional. Notice the personal items, but don't ask about them right away. Don't force the personal. Let it happen. If the customers lead you that way, go with it. Otherwise, stay focused on the reason you're there in the first place, and that's to introduce yourself and your business offerings. Once you've truly connected, the conversation will undoubtedly drift into personal areas, but let it happen naturally.

Tip 4. Take Charge by Asking Questions

The fourth tip buyers are taught is to *take charge by asking the questions*. The strategy behind this is for the buyers to be on the offensive and force the salespeople to be on the defensive.

The buyers don't do it to be antagonistic but rather to maintain control. It always reminds me of the episode of the old TV show *Seinfeld* in which George dates a woman and tries desperately to have "hand." Both he and his girlfriend vie for who will have the upper hand in the relationship.

Ideally, in a mutually prosperous relationship, no one has the upper hand, but in this early stage of selling, the person who asks the questions is usually the one who can dictate the action. However, it's not because doing the talking is power. It's quite the opposite. Listening is much more powerful and persuasive than talking. That's why asking the questions is crucial.

I believe there is a direct correlation between how much the customers talk and the probability of making a sale. This is really Relationships 101. The more they talk and the salespeople listen, the higher the odds of building trust and a solid relationship.

This was solidified many years ago after having a conversation with my best friend, who happens to be a doctor. He was lamenting the fact that when a patient came into his office, he knew within seconds exactly what was wrong. After all, he said, "I've had years of training in my specialty and years of experience hearing how patients describe their pain. However, if I tell them right away what's wrong, they don't feel comfortable in my diagnosis. They want a second opinion. But if I spend 15 minutes listening to them without saying a word, even though I already know what's wrong, they are totally comfortable with my diagnosis and don't need any other opinions. I don't get it: They wait long to see me. Don't they want to get out as quickly as possible?"

I just smiled because I knew he had stumbled on a big rapport building secret. Everyone's favorite subject is himself or herself. Ask the questions and let the customers talk themselves right into your arms, figuratively, of course.

Tip 5. Downplay Your Needs

The fifth buying tip is to *downplay your needs*. Buyers are taught to minimize their needs in an attempt to get the salespeople to think smaller instead of bigger. This is the perfect example of why it's crucial to take charge of the sales call. Once the salespeople give up control of the sales call, they relinquish the role of being the experts.

Whenever customers tell you what they need, it is imperative that you never take their word for it. I don't suggest that you be dismissive of the things they say, but after all, you are the expert in what you sell, not them. What would your doctor say if you walked into her office and began to tell her what was wrong with you? Would she take your word for it? Of course not! She might ask for your input and ask about symptoms, but the final diagnosis is all hers. She's the expert.

Whenever you take the customers' word for what they need, you not only give up being the expert but you also slip a few notches on the customers' credibility scale. Customers love it when their salespeople take pride in what they sell and know their stuff. This is an opportunity. Don't blow it by being an order taker.

Tip 6. Ask About Price Right up Front

The sixth buying tip is one of the most common tricks in the buyers' arsenal, and that is to *ask about price right up front*. Sometimes even before saying hello, as if it were part of an automatic reflex, the buyers ask you about price. How you answer them at this critical juncture will set the stage for the rest of the interaction.

There are two distinctly wrong ways to answer. The first, of course, is to quote a price. Resist the temptation to give them a price no matter how simple it may seem or how proud you may be of a low price. You have given no information at this point, and quoting a price will only negate any other feature or benefit and put the entire focus on money. You may think you're saving time and getting straight down to business, but talking about price too soon is not only bad business but also bad for the relationship. It's out of order.

How would you feel if you were on a first date with someone, and 10 minutes into the date she asked you how much money you make? You would probably feel a little defensive. It's not that it's a bad question. If you had been dating that person for a while, it's a perfectly legitimate question and conversation to have. The problem is that a first date is not the right time to discuss such personal information. It's out of order. So is talking about price before you've done any fact-finding and given a presentation.

In fact, I prefer to not even get into price on the first visit if at all possible. Set up a follow-up appointment so you have time (or at least give the illusion) to customize your recommendation and price quote. It will make your customers feel special that you have thought about their needs before giving a recommendation. Prescription without diagnosis is malpractice every time.

The other wrong way to answer the upfront price question is with a range. Many salespeople think they are being clever by answering the buyers' question by giving them a range of prices. They feel that they can answer without getting specific. There's only one hitch to that philosophy: I have never seen a salesperson quote a price range without the customer's automatically focusing on the lower end of the range! You may say, "Our prices range from $99 to $500 depending on the package you select." The customers hear only $99. Now you've got to swim up stream. You'd be better off to quote only the upper end of the range and then pleasantly surprise your customers if you can save them money. The danger with doing this, however, is that they shut down literally and emotionally if they feel like they can't afford what you've quoted.

Even though it may create a bit of an awkward situation, you are infinitely better off not to answer the price question up front. Don't ignore it, but rather, address it in general terms by saying something like "I am more than eager to discuss our prices with you since I believe we are the best value in the industry, but before I do, I need to learn a little more about you and your needs." This maintains control and preserves order. If the buyers persist and continue to insist that you give a price, they may not be serious buyers or customers that you want to do business with. They may be just try-ing to get a price out of you to shop around and to go to another source.

Either way, you don't want to play this game. It's like someone's agreeing to go on a date with you only to make another person jealous. If that is your date's purpose, it's better that you find out before you spend too much time and effort on that person. If your customers insist on a price, give them one more answer to see if it will suffice. I suggest something like this: "Well, I will tell you this. We are not the cheap-est, but we are not the most expensive either. If we are not the exact right company and do not have the exact right products or services, there will be no charge at all." This isn't say-ing your products or services will be free, but it does let them know, in no uncertain terms, that if the two of you don't find the relationship mutually beneficial, you won't be doing busi-ness together! That should work, but if they continue to insist on a price up front, my advice is to walk away. Problem prospects will only become problem customers.

Tip 7. Flinch

The seventh buying tip is to *flinch*. This is as old as it gets. A flinch is when the buyers verbally or visually react when you quote a price. It may be a raise of the eyebrows, a scratch on the head, or a frown. They may say, "Ouch!" Whatever the flinch, you don't want to react. There's no need to respond to their theatrics. They didn't ask a question so there isn't anything to say.

It may be painful, but stay quiet, and whatever you do, don't ask a question. Do not say, "Is that too high for you?" or "What price were you expecting?" These responses play right into their hand and imply that you've got room for negotiation. Do not respond.

However, if you know your limitations and absolutely cannot stay quiet, there's only one response that won't do more harm than good and that's to flinch back. Flinch back by saying, "I can't believe our price is that low either!" If they chuckle, you've made your point. If they don't find humor in your reply, that's OK too. You're still better off than if you had said anything else.

Tip 8. Use the Word *Budget*

The eighth buying tip is the buyer's coup de grace. *Coup de grace* is a French expression meaning "the killing blow," and this tip is the one that usually deals the biggest blow to salespeople. The buying seminar leader said that this tip was to salespeople what kryptonite was to Superman. This tip is to *use the word* budget. Their thought, and a correct one I might add, is that most salespeople do not have any clue how to respond to that word.

I have asked thousands of salespeople in my seminars how they respond when buyers tell them that the price they quoted was "too high for their budget." The overwhelming response most salespeople give is, "What is your budget?" This is not only a weak response but it's also exactly what the buyers were hoping you'd say! By asking about their budget, you've implied that there is flexibility in your price, and the negotiating has begun. I'll even go as far as to say that I believe asking about a customer's budget is the absolute worst question salespeople can ask! A customer's budget should be completely irrelevant. I will illustrate why with another doctor example.

Let's say you went to see your doctor about stomach pain you've been having. After an examination, your doctor tells you that you need your appendix removed. She goes on to explain that this is no cause for alarm. She says, "This is a common procedure performed dozens of times each and every week. The only risk is waiting and doing nothing. If an appendix erupts inside, it will cause massive bleeding, and then it will become a major emergency. So scheduling the procedure to remove it should be done right away. But before we do, one last question: What's your budget?"

Stop for a second and think about how you might feel about your doctor's question. Budget might matter to you, but should it matter to the doctor? Shouldn't the doctor's only concern be how to make you well? Would you feel a bit uneasy with the mere suggestion that budget might matter to the doctor? I'll bet you would want your doctor focused on getting the job done and let you figure out how to pay for it. Doctors may have that conversation with an insurance company, but they shouldn't have it with patients. It's almost a conflict of interest. Fitting into a budget should not be their concern.

Same is true in selling. Budgets might matter to customers but not to any salespeople worth their salt. Your job as a salesperson is to get the job done. If the customers trust you and you've sold them sufficiently, they'll figure out how to pay for it.

For those of you who are mathematically oriented, here is a simple equation to further explain my point. If value is greater than price $(V > P)$, then budgets are irrelevant. Only if price is equal to or less than value ($P \leq V$) will budgets matter. The customers will continue to negotiate until value exceeds price. Of course, this will occur at the detriment of your profit margin.

Bottom line: Do your job and they'll find the money; otherwise, it will come out of your pocket.

Tip 9. Put off a Decision as long as Possible

The ninth buying tip is to *put off a decision as long as possible*. This is the dreaded stall. They won't make a decision if they don't have to, and most salespeople never give their customers a compelling reason to make a decision. In other words, they are not sold. Stalls come in many forms including "Let me think it over," "Let me run it by my boss," or "I'd like to sleep on it."

Assuming your customers have even a little interest in your product or service, the stall is a direct result of a poor sales job. There's no countermeasure to a stall except to attempt to find out what is preventing them from making a decision. It may be a good idea to schedule a follow-up meeting so you can have a chance to regroup and come back with something that will truly excite them. Translate a stall as a request for more information rather than as something negative. A stall means they haven't hit the right emotional hot button, and it's your job to find it. A stall is nothing more than a hiccup in the relationship if you handle it right and don't overreact.

Tip 10. Play off Your Competition

The last buying tip may be one of the most common, and that is to *play off your competition*. If you've been selling for more than three hours, undoubtedly you've run into this one. This is an attempt by the buyers to get a better deal from you by letting you know that your competition is offering a better price. This can be done subtly or overtly. It often sounds like this: "I'd love to work with you, but so and so if offering a lower price. If you match it, the business is yours."

This is when, although it will take all the willpower you can muster, you must **not** take the bait. First, it may or may not be true. Many times this is simply a negotiating tactic, and there really is no better deal from a competitor. Second, even if there is, by agreeing to match someone else's price, you are saying that there is no difference between you and your competitor. What should you do?

Glad you asked. I've got a response for you to use whenever this, or any other price objection, arises. When buyers tell you that a competitor is offering a better price, don't debate it with them. Simply respond by saying, "You are right! I have no doubt that they can give you a better price. But I can give you a better cost." Then sit back and watch their reaction. Chances are they will look puzzled and ask you what you mean.

This is your second-chance opportunity to completely sell them, and you had better have an answer ready to go. You first need to understand the difference between price and cost. I don't mean what you think I might mean. I don't mean price is a retail figure and cost is a wholesale figure. I mean that price is just a number. Whatever it is, it's a numerical figure. Cost encompasses more than just a number. It takes into account all the factors that go into the product or service. Cost is an emotional figure.

A perfect analogy is the way my father shops. He is the kind of guy who will drive across town to buy a case of Coca-Cola that is $2 cheaper than the store around the corner. My father gets a lower price, but he pays a higher cost. Once you factor in gas, wear and tear, time, and effort, he pays a higher cost.

Almost without exception, those items with a lower price also have a higher cost, and those with a higher price, cost less in the long run. You must have a response ready to fire as to why you have the lower cost. Cost is where you want to compete, not price. Another word for cost is *value*. Having the lowest price may help complete a transaction, but having the best value will ensure a customer for life.

You can use the price versus cost comparison whenever price comes up. If I'm at the point where I am ready to discuss price but the customers jump the gun and ask me first, I like to say to them: "Before I give you my price, I need to know one more thing. Are you looking for a low price or low cost?" After they shake their head in bewilderment, I go on to explain how I am different from the competition and how I can provide more value. Sometimes I even use the example of my father in my explanation. Price versus cost is not a gimmick. Don't use it if you can't articulate real value differences. But if you can, this one technique will transform how you talk about money. You will not fear the price conversation but will look forward to it. You will be among those supersalespeople who ask sincerely, "What's all the fuss about price?!"

CHAPTER 8

From Captivation to Cultivation

Closing a sale is like popping the question. You wouldn't ask someone to marry you if you didn't expect her to say yes. You not only expect a positive answer but you plan for it as well. You expect a yes because the timing is right and both parties are ready to take the next step in the relationship. Selling should be the same way. Great salespeople *expect* people to do business with them. They expect to sell. Average salespeople hope to sell.

That seems like a minor difference, but it's actually quite significant. It is this quiet, but very evident, confidence that is contagious and is an unconscious factor in making the sale and building relationships. Even though you expect a yes, you still have to ask the question. You still should always ask for the business.

As I've stated before, closing should be the inevitable, logical next step in the relationship. If not, something went off track somewhere along the way. Just as if you asked someone to marry you and she said anything other than yes. There is a disconnect somewhere.

MOVING FROM CLOSING THE SALE TO CULTIVATING THE RELATIONSHIP

Nonetheless, when someone does agree to marry you, and when someone does agree to do business with you, it is the beginning of the relationship, not the ending. All too often, salespeople regard closing a sale as the proverbial end of the road instead of the beginning of a new road. They should not do that. Instead, closing a sale is where salespeople move from captivation to cultivation. Everything that took place up until closing was courtship. Now the real work of continuing to earn the customer's business and building trust and loyalty begins.

This begins a never ending cycle of reinforcing the decisions customers have made. While captivation is an event, cultivation is a process. Captivation is the process of courtship. Cultivation is the process of romance. Solid relationships never lose the romance. It is often a missing element in both personal and business relationships, but especially in business, but it shouldn't be. Salespeople spend enormous amounts of time and energy trying to make the sale and close the deal, only to ignore and jeopardize that relationship once it's made. A truly great salesperson must be equally good at both captivation and cultivation.

This hit home to me very early in my career. It was 1984, and I was selling yellow pages in the Washington, D.C., area. There was a particular customer in downtown D.C. whom I had been working with to get an appointment for months. He finally relented and agreed to see me. He said, "I'll see you tomorrow at six o'clock."

I replied, "OK, I am looking forward to it. See you tomorrow evening!"

He said, "Evening? No, I meant six o'clock in the morning."

Pretending not to gasp, I said, "Even better!"

Now, I have to admit that six o'clock in the morning was a little before my normal comfort zone. Not to mention that I lived in the suburbs, so this meant that I'd have to get up at four to leave by five o'clock. To top it off, it was February, and it was brutally cold, and I had to allow 15 minutes just to scrape my windshield!

Nevertheless, I did it, and I had a successful sales call resulting in a sale.

I remember leaving his office at 6:45, high as a kite, thinking, now what? Where was I to go next? It was too early to knock on doors, and even my office wasn't open yet. But something that customer said to me that morning has stuck with me all these years. He told me that he purposely sets all his appointments with salespeople at 6 a.m. for two reasons. He explained that he was a busy man and that early morning was the only time he wouldn't be interrupted by normal business activity. The second reason, he said, was that it was a good test of the salesperson's commitment. He went on to say that any salesperson who hems and haws or suggests an alternate time loses the chance to sell him forever. He said, "I don't want to sound harsh, but any salesperson who isn't willing to go the extra mile to make a sale will never be willing to go the extra mile once the sale has been made."

That was a lesson I have never forgotten. Once a sale has been made and commissions paid, former customers aren't as important to salespeople as the next prospects. They forget that former and current customers are excellent sources of new business and referrals, not to mention that it is infinitely cheaper to keep existing customers than it is to get new ones.

This is not to say that prospecting shouldn't be a priority and we shouldn't always be looking for new business. I am simply saying that salespeople shoot themselves in their own foot by thinking their job is done once they make a sale. When salespeople are responsive and attentive before the sale but then suddenly aren't as responsive and attentive after the sale, it leads to buyers' remorse and ill-will.

These disenfranchised customers often turn into problem customers and bad payers. Collection issues are often a result of neglected customers. Then, there's the adverse effect of negative word of mouth. It is well documented that a dissatisfied customer shares their unfavorable opinion with an average of 10 other people. And 1 in 5 tells 20 others. This can be avoided by realizing that every sales transaction is the beginning, not the end, of a new relationship. Customer service is not someone else's responsibility. It is the salesperson's job, and it begins right after the customer has signed on the dotted line.

THE FIVE BE-STRATEGIES

There's an age-old saying that has a bearing here: "If you are not willing to take care of your customer, someone else will." You can bet that there are other salespeople just waiting in the wings for you to stumble. While you can never fully insulate your customers from the competition, there are things you can do to keep from losing them. You are not helpless. In the following section, we will look at the things that are necessary to do in order to cultivate a business relationship and competition proof your customer. I call them "Be-Strategies" because they are all proactive cultivation strategies that start with "be."

Be-Strategy 1. Be Friends

We've talked about it before, but being friends with your customers is the single most important theme of this entire book, and it is the single most important thing you can do to create loyal customers. Friendship has no middle ground. Either you are friends, or you're not. There certainly are varying degrees of friendship, but the alternative to being friends is being just a vendor.

A vendor or supplier is someone the customers do business with. The relationships are purely platonic, and they often revolve around whether or not you can give the customers the best deal monetarily. When salespeople are nothing more than vendors, there is no emotional investment or connection to the salespeople. Customers are doing business with you solely because they want your product or service, and you are irrelevant and inconsequential. This is not where any salesperson wants to be. As a professional salesperson, you should want to matter!

For you to have any shot at cultivating loyalty, you must have some emotional connection with your customer. It may not be as full-blown friends, but you are important to them in some way. Perhaps it's because they want and respect your input and proactively seek your advice, or maybe it's because they find you uplifting and inspiring to be around. Whatever the reason, there must be an emotional connection that transcends the buying transaction.

I've frequently used the following test in my seminars to determine whether or not customers view salespeople as vendors or friends: How many invitations do you get to your customers' company events, such as holiday parties, summer barbecues, brainstorming sessions, team building events, and birthday and/or retirement gatherings? If the answer is none or very few, you probably don't have quite as loyal customers as you might have thought. These invitations are indications that you are thought of outside the selling and buying process. They indicate willingness on the part of your customers to expand the relationship and become better connected. These invitations are a good gauge of your customers' emotional investment and whether they consider you to be their friend. Maybe not the kind of friend they call late in the evening when they have a personal crisis, but a friend nonetheless. It's a notch up the relationship totem pole.

The deeper the connection and the more value you bring to the table, the stronger the loyalty will be. Loyalty across industry lines is at an all-time low, and a large part of that has occurred because we have gotten so transaction oriented and we either don't care or know how to build relationships anymore. That's unfortunate because without a true relationship, you can make a sale, but you will never develop an account.

Average salespeople make sales. Great salespeople build accounts that they can count on for business over and over again. If all you do is make sales, you will have to work twice as hard to continue making new sales because there is no repeat business, referral business, or account penetration. Once you have closed the deal and made the sale, celebrate. But then immediately shift into friend building mode. Not only will this help prevent buyers' remorse but it will also solidify in the customers' mind that you will be around when they need you.

Do the kind of things friends do: call to check in with them with no other motive; clip and e-mail articles and stories to them that might be of interest to them; and get a little personal information if possible. Don't immediately pull out a pad and start asking in-depth personal stuff like where they live and how many kids they have. That might scare them. It would me. Don't force being friends; just be open to it. Find out when their birthday is and their anniversary on the job. These aren't too personal, and they are appropriate to new friendships.

Relationships must progress on their volition and timetable, so be open and ready and let it happen. Otherwise, you'll just be their vendor, and that should be unacceptable to any professional salesperson.

Be-Strategy 2. Be an Expert

You can go a long way toward cultivating friendships with customers by demonstrating your expertise and familiarity with their industry. The more of a resource you can become to your customers, the more indispensable you will be.

Knowledge can be the ultimate competitive advantage that keeps your customers loyal. Whenever possible, but especially for those customers that you cannot afford to lose, immerse yourself in their world. Subscribe to and read their own company newsletters and trade publications and attend their industry's events whenever possible. The more of an insider you can become, the more valuable you will be to them. There is also a secondary benefit of becoming an industry expert, and that's the increased business that goes along with it. Let me share a story about my journey as a staffing industry expert.

It was 1992, and I had been speaking for a living for six years. I got a call from a woman who ran a staffing company in the Washington, D.C., who wanted me to speak at a small industry event. After a successful presentation, she invited me to run some training sessions for her sales staff. That went so well the company signed me to a two-year training contract. In those two years I got to know the industry so well that I was asked to contribute articles to the staffing industry's trade publications. Upon seeing my articles, I got calls from several other staffing companies and associations.

Well, let's fast-forward to the present day. I am considered a staffing industry expert, having made hundreds of industry presentations and consulted with too many companies to count. I have turned down offers to become an industry executive!

Many years since 1992, the staffing industry has accounted for half of all the speaking engagements for the entire year. I can't say that I set out to become a staffing expert; it just happened. But I am sure glad it did.

Be-Strategy 3. Be Loyal

It's ironic that we are exploring ways to keep our customers loyal to us when two of the major causes of customer disloyalty is disloyalty and lack of integrity on the part of salespeople. Nothing can doom a relationship faster than if trust has been breached.

We know this to be true of personal relationships. A couple can withstand a lot of setbacks and disappointments and still stay together, but a breach in trust is hard to get past. Same is true with business relationships. Somehow we mistakenly believe that trust is not as important in business relationships as it is in our personal lives, but people are people. Just because the setting is an office building as opposed to a residence doesn't change the fact that there are people inside both. As I've said over and over, the same rules apply. Trust is critical to any and all relationships!

So how might a salesperson lose the trust of the customer? Well, that could happen by any number of ways, but there are two ways it happens most often. The first is by not keeping your word. Many times this occurs quite innocently. It isn't intended, but the effects are the same as if it were intentional. For example, have you ever been late for an appointment? Have you ever had to reschedule an appointment? Have you ever told a little white lie to a customer? Have you ever stretched the truth a bit about your company's policies or services? Have you ever told customers you'd have an answer for them by noon but didn't get to calling them until late afternoon? All of these chip away at trust. All of these lead to less loyalty.

To underscore the importance of keeping your word, all you need to do is relate it to a personal situation. How would you feel if someone were late for a first date or had to reschedule? How would you feel if someone told you she'd call by a certain time but she didn't call until several hours later? You might be saying that those are different situations, but they are not. Business relationships might be a little more tolerant, but the human reactions and consequences are exactly the same. If you want honesty and loyalty from your customers, you must give them honesty and loyalty first! It reminds me of a song by Seals & Crofts (I know I am really showing my age) that says, "Darling, if you want me to be closer to you, get closer to me." This was good advice then, and it's good advice now.

The second way of breaking trust is by not having price integrity. Not much attention is ever paid to price integrity, but I believe it's a bigger issue than anyone realizes. Price integrity is violated when you arbitrarily charge different prices to different customers for the same product or service. Unfortunately this happens all too frequently. It may seem harmless enough and easy to justify, and for the most part, no one ever finds out. I've even caught myself charging one fee to one client and another fee to someone else.

I better clarify. The harm isn't that you have multiple fees. You can make your pricing scheme as complicated as you want. The harm is when you're not consistent in the application of those fees. I chose several years ago to charge more when I had to travel farther: the closer to home, the lower the fee. I had different rates for all four time zones and a special rate for those within driving distance.

There is nothing unethical about any of this. The problem occurs if I give different fees to customers within the same time zone or fee bracket. I may be able to justify it somehow, but I run the—albeit very small— risk of my customers' finding out and feeling cheated. Even if they never find out, I've still broken the Golden Rule of doing unto others as I would want others to do unto me. It's not right, and it's no way to treat a friend.

So, am I saying that negotiating in any fashion is harmful to the relationship? No. But it can be harmful if you apply your pricing rules arbitrarily. There is one way to escape this pricing conundrum, and that's to have a concession policy. You should always try to apply pricing consistently, but if and when you need to charge a lower price to one customer over another, make sure you get a concession for every price reduction you give. For instance, if your price is $100 for a set of widgets but the customers are willing to pay only $80, you can maintain price integrity by agreeing to the $80 in exchange for a concession on their part. They might give you 10 referrals, agree to shorter terms, or give you $20 of advertising in their company newsletter. This way you are not arbitrarily discounting but rather getting full price because they made up the difference with their concession. The rule of negotiating should always be that when you make a concession, get a concession of equal value in return. You maintain price integrity and never have to worry that other customers might somehow find out.

Be-Strategy 4. Be Willing to Go the Extra Mile

It happens to almost all relationships over time. We start to take the other person for granted. We stop doing the little things that made our partners fall in love with us. The romance wanes. It happens in personal relationships, and it happens in business.

Salespeople are attentive and at their best when chasing a sale, only to seemingly disappear once the sale has been made. I talked about this earlier in this chapter, but lack of attention after the sale is an all too frequent happening. Many salespeople seem to not understand that customer service is part of a salesperson's job. I once overheard a salesperson for a Fortune 500 company tell a customer that he didn't handle customer concerns and issues. "That," he said, "was the role of customer service."

While I concede that company's have a customer service department to help keep salespeople selling and not get bogged down with too many service-related issues, anything that pertains to their customer should be of importance to the salespeople! I find fault with the attitude, not the procedure, of turning it over to customer service. When the customers start to feel unappreciated, they begin to look elsewhere. They can get over the physical mistake; it's the emotional disappointment that does the damage.

Going the extra mile sometimes means taking the time to listen and make the customers feel special. It's all about feelings. Going the extra mile has no specific rules or suggested things to do. It's often spontaneous and individualized for each unique customer and situation. Know what things are important to your customers and what makes them feel special and then do them. Handwrite thank-you notes instead of using a form letter, and drop in every now and then just to say hello. It's always the little things that make the biggest difference.

Be-Strategy 5. Be There

Whoever said that absence makes the heart grow fonder didn't know much about cultivating relationships. Sure, it's nice to get a break from your relationship every now and then, but any prolonged absence will do far more harm than good.

People are designed to need other people. Customers are people too. The single biggest telltale sign that you might be losing an account is if it's been a long time since you've heard from a customer. There is a direct correlation between the amount of time since you've been face-to-face and how strong and competition proof the relationship is.

This isn't to say that you should smother your customers with your neediness. There sometimes is a fine line between stalking and cultivating. Assuming you know the difference and take your cues from other person, there is no substitute for regular contact and timely follow-up. In other words, just be there. And when you're together, be there as well. Don't your mind wander and miss the opportunity to be in the moment. Customers can tell when your mind is elsewhere, and it can be damaging to the relationship.

Bottom line: A strong customer relationship is not a destination; it is an ongoing journey. Selling is two-part process, captivation and cultivation.

Captivation is making the sale and getting a customer. Cultivation is keeping that customer and strengthening the connection. Cultivation, like personal romance, takes time, and it never ends.

CHAPTER 9

Cultivating Through Crisis

Let's face it, it's easy to build a relationship when the sun is shining, everyone loves you, and there's not a cloud in the sky. It's an entirely different matter when things go wrong. And in the ever changing world of business, things can and do go wrong. In this chapter, we will explore how to continue to move the relationship forward when the customer has a complaint and how to steer clear of the bumps in the road that could threaten to end even the best of relationships.

The one thing you can bank on is that there will be problems. No relationship has ever existed that didn't experience some setbacks. Sometimes the problems are brought on by the salesperson, and sometimes they are caused by someone or something else. Either way, they happen, and the customer is upset. However, problems are rarely the thing that dooms the relationship. It's almost always how the problem is handled. Ineffective, insincere crisis management will do more harm than the crisis itself. The same is true of overreactions to a problem. Those responses are unfortunate because problems are nothing more than opportunities.

Somewhere along the way, we've come to believe the mistaken notion that customer problems and complaints are bad. The exact opposite is true. Most complaints and grievances are never verbalized. They remain unspoken, and the relationship just drifts apart, usually to the surprise and bewilderment of the salesperson. According to a study done by Lee Resource, Inc., (http://customerservice manager.com/customer-service-facts.htm) for every 1 customer who verbalizes a complaint, there are 26 other customers who had the same complaint but remained silent. This is, of course, an average that varies from industry to industry, but even if the silent part is cut in half, it's still a significant statistic.

The fact that the overwhelming majority of all customer complaints never get verbalized should be very humbling to any sales or customer service person reading this, and it should fundamentally change the way we handle complaints. Instead of thinking of problems and complaints as negative and as distractions, think of them as positive and as opportunities. If it's not the problem itself that dooms a relationship and if most problems and complaints are never made known to the salesperson, getting a verbalized complaint is a very rare opportunity. We need to think of the complainers as being more precious than gold! For more customer service statistics and information, visit http://www.customer1.com/blog/customer-service-statistics.

We put more emphasis on the customers we never hear from than we do on the customers we do hear from. We perceive the vocal customers as high maintenance and always complaining, but this is often a mistake. When customers take the time to complain, they are subconsciously letting us know that they value the relationship and want to make amends. It may be hard to see that because they are acting out of frustration and disappointment, but they wouldn't even bother complaining if they didn't care.

We know this to be true from our personal relationships. Love and anger are not diametrically opposed to each other. They are actually quite similar emotions. The people we care about the most are the ones that can upset us the most. People we don't care about can't upset us. There's no emotional connection. On the other hand, the opposite of love and caring is apathy. We don't get upset because we simply don't care. So the irate and complaining customers are the ones that really care, and the customers you never hear from are neutral and apathetic. Of course, you should always be striving to move every relationship forward and to get those apathetic customers to be emotionally invested, but the complaining customers should always take priority.

These customers are opportunities that should not be missed. Research finds that customers are up to four times more likely to remain loyal when they experience a problem that is handled properly than if there has never been any problem at all. If you quickly, effectively, and professionally take care of customers' complaints, you will propel the relationships forward faster than almost any other single activity. Effective crisis management breeds loyalty, but it also is true in reverse. Poor handling of a complaint breeds resentment and will end a relationship faster than any single activity.

FOUR STEPS IN HANDLING CUSTOMERS' COMPLAINTS

It's in every sales or customer service person's best interest to know exactly how to handle a customer complaint. I believe the four steps described in the following paragraphs will diffuse customer anger and effectively handle most problematic situations.

Step 1. Say "Thank You"

The first step is to always say "Thank you!" These should be the very first words out of your mouth in response to any complaint regardless of how big or small the complaint. This of course is not easy, especially if your customer is less than hospitable on the other end. However, be certain, sincere, and emphatic as to what you're thanking them for. You are thanking them for the opportunity. You are thanking them for bringing the problem to your attention. You are thanking them for allowing you the chance to rectify their complaint and for the courtesy of sharing their thoughts. The alternative is that they say nothing, stew over it, and ultimately do business with someone else. Another reason for thanking them right up front is that it diffuses the situation. It takes away some of their angst.

One of the main reasons only 1 in 26 customers complain is because no one likes confrontation, and that's exactly what the customers expect when they raise an issue. They expect the sales or customer service people to get defensive and that the net result will be an escalation of the crisis. Greeting their complaint with a sincere thank you will immediately take some of the venom out of their sting. As with all words, however, the magic is not in the words but rather how you say them. An insincere or monotone, robotic thank you will backfire and cause them to be more resolute in the complaint.

Step 2. Own the Problem

The second step in crisis management is to own the problem and apologize for the inconvenience. This is also meant to remove some of their angst. They are expecting the sales or customer service people to make excuses, cover their butts, and pass the buck. Letting them know up front that you are going to own the problem will almost immediately pay dividends. I've witnessed a customer's entire demeanor dramatically change in just a few seconds.

The key to this step is that it is tied at the hip with step 1 with no pause in between. For example, "Thank you so much, Bob, for bringing this to my attention and allowing me the opportunity to see what I can do to help. I apologize for any inconvenience this may have caused." Notice that there is no gap or hesitancy between steps 1 and 2. They are two distinct elements but part of one upfront disclaimer. Notice also that this is not a personal apology. It is a professional apology. You are not saying you are personally responsible or assigning blame anywhere for that matter. You are merely apologizing that they endured the inconvenience of the problem. After all, you may not be to blame. Your company may not be to blame. It could have been their fault!

The only time you should make a personal apology is if you actually are responsible for the problem. Then it's OK to say, "I'm sorry." Otherwise, apologize for the inconvenience. Assigning blame or trying to figure out who is to blame is the biggest waste of time and crisis escalator that you could do. The customers don't care whose fault it is; they only care about what's going to happen next. Later on you can figure out what happened, but don't do it in the heat of the moment with your customers.

Step 3. Allow Customers to Fully Dump Their Bucket

The third step in crisis management is to allow the customers to fully "dump their bucket." This is often referred to as DTB. This is where you get them to fully vent. There is a direct relationship between how much they dump from their bucket and how amenable they will be to accepting your resolution. The more you can get them to talk and vent, no matter how painful this might be, the more likely it is that you will resolve things amicably.

Although I've listed this as step 3, DTB can occur at step 1. For instance, some customers will be in full-dump mode the second you pick up the phone. When this happens, let them go. Let them get it all out. The last thing you want to do is interrupt them to say thank you and apologize for the inconvenience. Those steps can occur after they've vented. Also, some customers will vent easily and freely, while others will need a little help. You may need to ask a few questions to encourage them to vent. Something as simple as "Please start at the beginning, and tell me everything that has happened while I take a few notes" may be all that is needed to tilt their bucket. It really doesn't matter when they dump their bucket; it only matters that they do.

Complaints are emotional and personal. They are never platonic and logical. They happen because people feel slighted and let down. Therefore, you must handle the complaints emotionally instead logically. Reasoning and dissecting where things went wrong is handling complaints with logic. The same is true with trying to calm them down or fighting anger with anger. Let them vent. It is only after they've had their say that they will begin to settle down and think rationally again.

Step 4. Attempt to Achieve Resolution

The last step in dealing with a crisis is the attempt at resolution, whatever that may be. The resolution is when you tell them what you are going to do next, or better yet, when you ask them what they want you to do next.

One of my favorite examples of a calming, conciliatory resolution question is to ask customers, "What do you think is a fair resolution?" Instead of your telling them what you'll do, you're asking them for their input. After all, customers are just fighting for what they think is fair, and 75 percent of the time they will give you an answer that is less than what you were willing to do in the first place. This is win-win.

Resolving the problem is important, but more than that, customers just want to be listened to and feel like they matter. Asking for their input is a great way to come to an agreeable resolution. Then, if you can fix the problem right then and there, do it. If you are able, and the situation calls for it, to offer some kind of concession, do it. If you are not able to resolve the problem right then and there, let them know immediately and tell them what you will do next in the attempt to resolve their issue.

That's why I say "attempt"—because the resolution may not be something you directly control. You may need other people's approval or their involvement. Remember, you own the problem regardless of whether other people must get involved. If, as part of the attempt at resolution, you must transfer customers to coworkers, there is a specific way to do that so it doesn't cause a flare-up in their anger.

Flare-ups and escalations of the problem occur when customers have dumped their bucket and have begun to settle down only to be blindly transferred to another person such that they must completely start over. Worse yet, they get transferred and get someone else's voice mail. When this happens, all the goodwill and trust that you've built up through your listening and allowing them to vent is flushed down the tubes, and you've legitimately given them something else to be mad at. The proper way to transfer customers is to ask if they mind holding (we'll cover later in this chapter the rules for putting customers on hold), while you get the other person on the line and fully explain your customers' complaint to that person.

It is your responsibility to brief your co-workers on your customers' behalf. Never make your customers repeat their complaints to other people.

Then before you connect your customers with other people, make sure those other people have the time, authority, and willingness to get involved. It is never good to have to transfer customers more than one time. If the people you need to get involved are unavailable, don't make the customers have to call back. Own the problem by following up with your coworkers when you can and then call the customers back yourself and repeat the steps above.

Be as specific as possible in everything you say. Ambiguity will almost always lead to further problems. If you tell your customers you will call them back with an answer by noon, make sure you do. If you still don't have an answer by noon, call your customers anyway and give them a new estimated time for an answer. The attempt at resolution is more important than the resolution itself. Customers want and need to know you care and that you are on their side. Sometimes problems can't be resolved, but your "attempt" is enough to win the customers' continued business.

~

I realize that following these four steps will not resolve every crisis. Problems, like relationships, can be very complex. Rather, I am suggesting that following these steps will give you a plan that will allow you to remain calm and in control. By owning the problem and being willing to listen, you will be able to earn the trust and confidence of your customers even if a mutual resolution isn't achieved. Not all problems are neatly resolved with a bow on top, but whether or not the problem dooms the relationship is entirely based on how you handle the problem.

With all that said, the last thing you want to do is be the cause of a customer complaint or letdown. Problems are stressful to relationships whenever they happen through the course of everyday business, but you, or someone else in your company, should never be the culprit. But that's exactly what happens all too often. Sales and customer service people unwittingly say and do things that put kinks in the relationship armor. As is true of any relationship, it's the littlest of things that others latch on to. A word or phrase here or there that is said quite innocently becomes a thorn in the relationship. Words, more than anything else, have incredible power that is capable of propelling a relationship forward or grinding it to an abrupt halt.

THE 10 WORST THINGS YOU CAN SAY TO CUSTOMERS

With this in mind, I've come up with what I call "The 10 Worst Things You Can Say to Customers." Some apply to just salespeople, others apply to just customer service reps, one or two apply to management, and a few apply to all of the above. For added drama, I'll count them down à la David Letterman style. Do I hear a drumroll?

The Tenth Worst Thing You Can Say: "I'm Sorry, What Was Your Name Again?"

This implies one of two things, and both are equally as bad. First, it could mean that they've given you their name but you can't remember it, or it could mean that they never told you because you didn't care to ask. If the focus is truly on building a relationship and not on completing a transaction, getting and remembering a customer's name should be the very first priority!

The Ninth Worst Thing You Can Say: "I'll Get to That as soon as Possible."

This may seem harmless enough, but it's the root cause of many business misunderstandings. The culprit is "as soon as possible," or ASAP as we often say. The problem with ASAP is that it gives the customers no specifics. There's way too much room for misinterpretation and ultimately disappointment. Does "ASAP" mean within a few minutes, a few hours, or a few days? It could be any of the above, and it is highly subjective. The remedy is to always give customers a quantifiable time frame and then be true to your word.

The Eighth Worst Thing You Can Say: "It Wasn't My Fault."

You may have to cover your you-know-what behind the scenes with your boss, but your customers don't care. Saying "It wasn't my fault" just makes you look petty and self-serving. I've said it before and can't say it enough: customers don't care who is to blame for a problem; they only care what you're going to do about it.

The Seventh Worst Thing You Can Say: "Please Hold."

This one is similar to ASAP. It doesn't give customers any options, and it doesn't tell them how long they can expect to be on hold. Studies show that customers begin to get irritated after just 17 seconds of being on hold if they were not informed of how long to expect to wait. The proper way to put someone on hold is to say, "Mr. Customer, to find out the answer, I will need to put you on hold for one minute. Is that OK? Or should I call you back?" This gives them options, and it allows them to make an informed decision because they know what to expect. If you take this step, they most likely won't mind being on hold because it was *their* choice. However, do not exceed the time you told them. If you said one minute, make sure you use an egg timer if necessary to not exceed what you've told them. It's always better to say longer and get to them quicker than to say shorter but take longer. In other words, underpromise and overdeliver.

The Sixth Worst Thing You Can Say: "You'll Have to Call Back Later."

There are so many things wrong with this brief sentence that I don't know where to begin. First, you never want to put the burden on them. If they are your customers, they are your responsibility. They don't have to do anything. They can go elsewhere. The old saying is true: "If you're not willing to take care of your customers, someone else will." Second, it's a statement with highly emotional overtones. It's weak and lazy, and it will cause your customers to think you're not really on their team. Relationships are two-way streets, and sometimes you need to go out of your way to take care of the other person.

The Fifth Worst Thing You Can Say: "I'm Sorry, but That Is Our Company Policy."

This may be the biggest scapegoat in business today! "Company policy" has been the culprit for more ruined relationships than almost any other single factor. Company policy in the hands of many sales and customer service people can be like putting a gun into the hands of Wyatt Earp from the wild, Wild West. I guess I should explain. It's not that I am against having company policy. Companies need policy to administer equality and maintain standards. I get it.

However, there are two inherent problems that often come with it. First, it becomes the easy way out. When a customer complaint, issue, or request becomes too burdensome or it seems unreasonable to the sales or customer service people, the easy way out is to hide behind company policy. For many reading this, your response may be "OK, so what? That's a good thing." While it may be an easy way out of the problem and may even save the company a few bucks, taking the easy road and not going to bat for the customers will almost always damage the relationship.

People and companies that make their money selling products and services wear two hats and have two allegiances. Yes, salespeople are technically employed by their company, but they also work for their customers. It's often a delicate balancing act. Customers believe you work for them, so when there's a problem, they at least expect you to go to bat for them. I believe that customer advocacy is the job of every sales and customer service person. It doesn't mean you'll solve every problem, nor does it mean that you should put your employment at risk, but your customers have every right to expect that you'll be empathetic and will make every attempt to make them happy.

The second inherent problem with hiding behind company policy is that it's often just bad policy. There is no way to verify this, but I am willing to bet that 90 percent of all company policies have been put in place to protect companies from being taken advantage of. That, of course, would be reasonable were it not be for the fact that we're talking about only a very small slice of the pie. Being conservative, fewer than 10 percent of customers try to get away with something or are dishonest. Most customers, the overwhelming majority, are good, decent, ethical, and honest. They are not trying to cheat the system. When you have a policy designed to protect yourself against the minority, it always handicaps and shortchanges the majority.

It's like when someone has had a bad previous personal relationship and you end up paying for it. The person doesn't want to get burned again so he or she protects himself or herself and doesn't trust you. What could have been a great relationship never has a chance because of a previous bad one. This hurts only the one doing the protecting, and the cycle continues. The same is true in business. When you penalize customers for the sins of previous customers, it sends a bad message and is bad business. Create policies for the majority, not the minority.

The Fourth Worst Thing You Can Say: "What's the Problem?"

How many times have you been greeted by someone, usually a manager or supervisor, with this one? The first thought through my head is that I don't have a problem. You do!

This question not only puts the other person on the defensive but it's also rude and tacky. It amazes me how often sales and customer service people say and do things that make customer complaints escalate. "What's the problem?" are fighting words and should never be used unless you simply don't care about the relationship. Asking "What's the problem?" may help you win the battle, but it may cause you to lose the war.

A good rule to live by is to calculate how much a typical customer is worth over the course of a lifetime. If the problem or discrepancy is not worth that amount, then be a little more humble and a little less defensive. It costs up to five times more to get a new customer than to keep an existing one, so don't be penny wise and pound foolish. Unless the customer is one of the very few who might be trying to cheat you in some way, it's better to use calming language than inflammatory language.

The Third Worst Thing You Can Say: "Do You Have a Coupon?"

This one isn't bad because of what it says but rather because of what it means. It is fine and dandy if customers do have a coupon, but if they don't, you are telling them that they are paying more than other customers.

This is not to say that I am against coupons. I am a big fan. What I am against is making customers feel unnecessarily slighted. Everyone understands how coupons work. Those who are avid coupon and bargain hunters can save a few dollars. But those who aren't don't want to be reminded that they're paying more.

Along the same lines is the statement, "We'll match any competitor's coupon or price." This too signals that other customers may be paying less. I believe it creates uneasiness and distrust, and it's just not good business. Accepting their coupon or matching a competitor's price tells the marketplace that there's no difference between you and your competitors. With that said, however, asking customers if they have coupons or bringing to their attention that they could have saved money is like dangling a carrot in front of them and then saying they can't have it. If they have a coupon, that's great. Otherwise, don't mention it.

The Second Worst Thing You Can Say: "I Could Get a lot More Work Done If Only Customers Would Stop Bugging Me!"

This one is an actual quote of a statement I overheard on the floor of a customer service department for a Fortune 100 company. It was so stunningly stupid that it immediately jumped to the top of this list. While I understood the sentiment, any company's worst nightmare is that customers will stop bugging them. Furthermore, any individual sales or customer service person's worst nightmare is for customers to stop bugging them.

The more customers need (and bug) us, the more job security we have. The fact is that sales and customer service people should hit their knees in thankfulness for every customer call and inquiry, good or bad. The alternative is unacceptable.

The Worst Thing You Can Say: "That's Not My Job" or "That's Not My Department."

If I had a dollar every time this was uttered, I'd be right up there with Donald Trump! Let me be as clear as possible: if it involves the customers, it's your job. Period. You may need to involve other people or other departments, but it's your responsibility to help them in whatever ways they need assistance. If you're going to say "It's not my job," you might as well just tell the customers that you could care less about their business. That's what they hear. They hear apathy, and apathy is the worst sin you can commit in a relationship.

I've talked about how the opposite of love is not hate. Love and hate are byproducts of caring. The opposite of love is apathy and indifference. The relationship is dead when one or both parties don't care anymore. Unless it is truly how you feel, you never want the other person to think you don't care, and that's exactly what your customers will think when they hear "It's not my job."

⌒

Bottom line: Now, I could easily have listed 50 dumb things to say, but a lot of them are offshoots of things already on this list. The bottom line is to Always Be Cultivating and to avoid saying and doing things that can derail the relationship's momentum.

Problems will arise, but if you see them for the opportunities they are and handle them with grace and humility, the relationships will not suffer. In fact, they will get stronger.

CHAPTER 10

The Sore-Thumb Principle

Hopefully, by now, you are convinced that every successful relationship has an order and rhythm of captivation and cultivation with the central ingredient being contagiousness. Being contagious is the necessary DNA of relationships in the twenty-first century.

Up until now, we've focused exclusively on the one-on-one relationship. However, there are relationships that go beyond the one-on-one experience.

INSTITUTIONAL RELATIONSHIPS

There are three other relationships that are crucial to business success. There is the relationship that companies have with the marketplace at large, the relationship that companies have with their employees, and the relationship that employees have with their employer. I call these *institutional relationships*, and just as with a one-on-one connection, being contagious is just as important. This global kind of contagiousness is achieved through something I call the *sore-thumb principle*.

The sore-thumb principle refers to the concept of sticking out like a sore thumb. When my kids were younger, they would have rather had their heads bitten off by a giant snake than to stick out from the crowd in any way. However, in the business world, being unique, authentic, and getting noticed (in a positive way) is the idea behind the sore-thumb principle, and it is something worth achieving.

The term *sore thumb* may be a bit unusual for business circles, but the concept is not. Just look at wildly loyal relationship that Apple has with its customers or that Google has with its employees. Customers have been known to wait in line for days, braving the elements, to be among the first to buy a new Apple product. I know people who would quit their jobs and work for free at Google, and we all know some workaholics who are completely in love with the company they work for.

SORE-THUMB OPPORTUNITIES IN INSTITUTIONAL RELATIONSHIPS

Let's look at the three types of sore thumbs in the context of institutional relationships and explore the whys and hows for each.

The Relationship Companies Have with the Marketplace

While there are many attributes, experiences, and strategies that a company can employ to build a positive sore-thumb relationship with the marketplace, I will address only three and focus on how they affect contagiousness: reputation, brand, and energy.

Any of the three could be books by themselves. I certainly will not do any of them full justice but will instead focus on the role they play in connecting with the marketplace. All three are larger-than-life qualities that can have a dramatic effect on the relationship. Let's start with reputation.

Reputation

Reputation is the big umbrella with almost everything else falling underneath. Conventional wisdom has always held that reputations take lifetimes to create but mere seconds to destroy. This is partly true and partly not true. Relationships can definitely be damaged in seconds with one bad interaction. However, reputations can also be restored, established, or solidified in seconds as well. No longer does it take years to build them or to change them.

The speed of business in the twenty-first century is much faster than it has ever been at any point in history. Reputations change in a blink of an eye, are highly personal, and they can and will fluctuate with each and every interaction. Reputations are won and lost with every day and with every transaction because they are more personal than ever before. Business is personal, and every relationship is personal. Since reputations are in the eye of the beholder, companies have the opportunity to shape their reputations and be contagious each and every time they have contact with a customer. Customer service departments need to think of themselves as PR departments and the guardians of their company's reputation.

Let me give you a firsthand example of just how fast and fragile reputations can be. I have a long-standing love/hate relationship with a certain airline. What I would say about how I feel about them depends on the last experience I had with them. Sometimes I get the red carpet treatment. I've had agents offer to upgrade me at no charge and go out of their way to help me reroute when needed. One time a pilot came back into the coach section and greeted me by name! But other times I've been treated as if I were bothering them by being on the flight. I've had bags that fit into their little baggage display, but as I entered the aircraft, these very same bags were taken from me unceremoniously and thrown into the cargo section. I've had agents talk to me as if I were a criminal and they were my parole officers. How I feel about this airline is incredibly subjective and can change by the minute. I am not alone. Most customers would say the same thing.

Today's customers are different animals from 25 years ago. The bar of service is higher than ever before, and when it isn't met, customers react negatively. When I get bad service from an airline, I don't kick and scream, but I do make sure my next audience hears about it.

Reputations are works in progress. They rise and fall with every customer, with every interaction. Your reputation (and relationship) is only as strong as the last experience. You're either contagious in a positive way or contagious in a negative way. You're either enhancing your reputation or harming it. You stand out in either a positive way or a negative way. Very few interactions are truly neutral. Sore thumbs can cut both ways. Great companies recognize this. Average companies don't get it.

Brand

There is much hoopla about branding. Every company should have a brand yet very few even know what that means. Simply put, having a brand is having a distinct, proprietary identity. Having a brand involves knowing who you are and what makes you unique, and it is being able to articulate that effectively to the marketplace. I believe the majority of companies would not pass that test, but those who do are infinitely more contagious than those who don't.

To identify a brand, companies need to complete the following sentence: "We stand out from the competition by being the only company to _____." This is the sore-thumb principle at its core. Identifying something that it does, has, or practices that is unique to the company is the most basic element in establishing a brand. Whatever makes a company stick out like a sore thumb is its biggest source of opportunity and the beginnings of a brand identity.

Sore thumbs are highly contagious. The marketplace admires and rewards innovation and uniqueness, and it penalizes companies that play follow-the-leader. Many companies make the often fatal mistakes of conforming to other companies and not being bold enough to exploit the things that make them unique.

I know we don't think of pop legend Elton John as a branding and marketing expert, but he once wrote a line in a song that is spot-on advice for companies wanting to build a contagious identity. The song was "Someone Saved My Life Tonight," and the line was "So save your strength and run the field you play alone." I know it's an unusual source of business wisdom, but it's quite sound advice. If companies would take the time to figure out what makes them unique and stand out from the crowd, they would run the field they play alone. They would stick out like a sore thumb!

Energy

Understanding the fragility of a reputation and building a brand are excellent avenues of creating institutional contagiousness, but both won't add up to a hill of beans if a company's energy doesn't live up to the incredibly high standards of today's consumers. Energy is the vibe a company exudes. Energy is best exemplified in the way a company handles the touch points of marketplace contact. *Touch points* are the moments in which companies have the opportunity to influence customers. It's where the rubber meets the road in institutional relationships. There are many points of intersection between companies and their customers, but the main ones are telephone greetings, websites, and advertising. I'll address each one briefly.

I don't know how I could quantify this statement, but in my experience 99 percent of all telephone greetings lack any positive energy. Companies miss a great opportunity for sore-thumb moments by mandating that their employees greet customers with a stale, uniform greeting and by not educating them on how crucial this touch point is. How someone answers the telephone speaks volumes as to a company's culture and commitment to its customers.

A contagious telephone greeting should create a spark. It should convey passion, sincerity, and a willingness to serve. This is a tall order but when achieved, it can be a tremendous sore thumb. A proper greeting should always contain a thank you, the name of the company, a curiosity building statement, the name of the person answering the phone, and an offer of service. The first part and last parts are obvious. They are necessary information that must be relayed to the caller.

The curiosity builder, along with the way the words are delivered, is the sore-thumb part. A *curiosity builder* is a statement that creates a little anticipation and excitement. An example: "Thank you for calling XYZ Corporation, where every customer is treated like family. My name is Zack Oliver. How may I be of service?" The phrase "where every customer is treated like family" creates curiosity and sets the stage for a positive interaction. Of course, this must be delivered with energy and sincerity and not sound robotic and uninterested.

Similarly, a company's Internet presence should also be curiosity invoking, exciting, easy to navigate, and full of energy. I am not a website expert, so I won't spend much time on it, but I know when a website stands out and when it doesn't. Your website is an opportunity to be a sore thumb, so make the most of it.

Finally, any advertising should follow the same rules. Advertising is one of the best ways to trumpet your sore thumb. This is not a book on advertising, but the one point I want to hammer home here is that all of these touch points should be consistent with one another. In advertising, it's not as much what you say as it is how many times you say it. Repetition and consistency are the keys to any effective advertising campaign. If you use a different message in every ad, you will diminish the advertising's effectiveness. However, if in every ad, you hammer home the same message of how you stand out like a sore-thumb, your rate of return will increase.

The Relationship Companies Have with Their Own Employees

The second sore-thumb opportunity exists in the way companies treat their own employees. Successful companies know the secret to success: happy employees almost always translate into happy customers. I am surprised that so many companies don't seem to get that. Companies spend enormous amounts of time, money, and effort on sales, marketing, and customer service, but they forget who is doing the selling, marketing, and servicing. That's unfortunate because there is a direct correlation between how employees feel about their company and how customers feels about that company. This shouldn't be a surprise. It's all about relationships, and relationships are all about feelings and feelings dominate actions.

There are myriad ways to stand out and build better employee morale, but I will focus on what I believe is the most important. That is education. Knowledge and motivation go hand-in-hand. They are linked together on the same pulley. The more knowledgeable people are, the more motivated they are. The less knowledgeable people are, the more they struggle with staying motivated. Motivated employees are more positive, energetic, productive, and above all, contagious! It is in every company's best interest to keep its employees happy, and there's no better way to do that than through education. It is also well documented that the companies who invest in educating their employees have lower turnover rates than those who don't.

I believe that all companies should be in the business of education first, and their industry second. Sadly, in too many instances, education is considered an unnecessary luxury. Sure, companies would like to invest more in education, but they think they can't afford it. I believe they can't afford not to put an emphasis on education. I heard a saying very early in my career that I loved, and it has stuck with me: "The only thing worse than training your people and losing them is not training them and keeping them!"

Fortunately, there are some inexpensive ways companies can help educate their employees. For example, companies can create *learning libraries*. Create a central place for books, old tapes and videos, CDs and DVDs, so that people can check them in and out for free. Providing this resource demonstrates the importance of ongoing education, but it puts the burden of responsibility on the employees to make use of the resources. To get the most out of such a resource, you can make it a condition for continued employment. You can also calculate merit and base pay increases using the amount of learning employees have taken advantage of. I've seen this done very successfully, and I have even seen companies require their employees to give oral reports on the books they've read. This builds presentation skills, confidence, and overall communication skills. It also creates a little excitement and added energy for the learning initiative. The employees may kick and scream at first, but after a while, they end up appreciating what the forced learning has done for them.

I don't believe you grow a business or grow a company. I believe you grow the people, and as a result of growing the people, the company grows. The most important job of sales and customer service managers and leaders is to grow their people.

Abe Lincoln once said, "There are only two things that change a person's life: the books you read and the people you meet." This is an incredibly profound truth. The only things that can truly alter one's course in life are the knowledge one acquires and the opportunities that come through meeting people. Begin putting a premium on education today. It will attract the cream of the crop talent, and it will be an investment that will pay huge dividends tomorrow.

The Relationship Employees Have with Their Employer

The third, and final, sore-thumb opportunity is the way employees feel about their employer and their jobs. As an employee, you can stick out like a sore thumb by becoming the leader and staying motivated on a daily basis. Staying motivated is arguably the single most important skill a salesperson could acquire. I call it a *skill* because it can be learned. Nothing happens if you can't get and stay motivated. It is the root of all success, thus worth exploring a little deeper.

There are three big myths about motivation that must be exposed if we want to gain a better understanding of how to stay motivated.

Myth 1. Motivation Is an Effect, Not a Cause

Most people mistakenly believe that motivation happens as a result of something else happening first. This couldn't be further from the truth. Motivation is a cause, not an effect. Motivation always happens in advance of something good. Motivation happens first. It precedes results.

While some might argue that motivation can happen after a result, for example, after a big sale, I would counter that by saying it is extremely rare, and if that's the philosophy you're operating under, you'll need amazing patience! You might feel motivated after a big sale, but if you're not motivated beforehand, those big sales will be few and far between. You can control your own destiny by becoming motivated first and then reaping the benefits that will bring.

Myth 2. You Can't Control Motivation

Many people think of motivation as some abstract thing that comes and goes like a summer breeze. To believe this, one might think of motivation as something external or out of our direct control. The truth is that motivation is internal and something we have direct control over.

Motivation is a choice. For example, we've already discussed how reading and continued learning can help get and keep you motivated. Well, that is a choice. You must choose to do that if you want the reward. Associating with positive people can also help keep you motivated. This is a choice. Avoiding negative self-talk and doubt can help keep you motivated. Don't take part in the negative banter around the water cooler. Being positive, using encouraging, uplifting language, and practicing optimism all are choices. Exercise has also been proven to increase self-esteem and release endorphins throughout your body. Endorphins are the chemical neurotransmitters produced by the pituitary gland that promote a feeling of well-being and exhilaration. All of the above produce endorphins, but all are choices. They don't happen on their own. Action creates motivation.

In fact, I often speak on the amazing power of taking action to change the way you think. We've all heard of *psychosomatic conditions*. Basically, these are the result of the power of mind over matter. The Greek word *psycho* means "mind" and *soma* means "body." *Psychosomatic* means that something originated in the mind and went to the body. It isn't an imaginary condition. It is a real condition. But it started in the mind. Well, I also believe in *somapsychotic conditions*. This is the exact opposite. This is changing the way you think and feel by taking action first. It's matter over mind! If you don't like the mental condition you're in, change it by engaging in physical action. Force yourself to take a walk. Force yourself to make that extra phone call or stop in on one last customer. It will get those endorphins flowing, and it will have an incredible effect on the way you feel.

Myth 3. Motivation Is Just Fluffy Stuff

Motivation is often referred to as a "soft skill." The implication is that it's not an incredibly vital skill, if it's even a skill at all. The thought is wrong on both counts. First, motivation is a skill. A skill is something that can be learned and something that can be harnessed when needed, and motivation meets those criteria. As with all skills, some people are more naturally predisposed than others, but I have seen people learn to be motivated to do things that they didn't like to do, thus dispelling the notion that you have to love something to be motivated about doing it. It's certainly preferable and considerably easier to get motivated if the desire is there, but it can be learned without it.

Some people would define a *soft skill* as "a skill that is not crucial" and a *hard skill* as "a skill that is complex and crucial." Given those meanings, I would dispute with as much vigor as I could muster the notion that motivation is a "soft skill." I would argue that motivation is the hardest skill of all. Motivation is both complex and critical. It is the skill of all skills in the sense that without it no other skill matters.

If a surgeon is brilliant in the operating room but not motivated to be there, would you want him or her to operate on you? I would bet not. If an athlete has all the God-given tools one would need to perform at the highest level but is not motivated to play, how far will he or she go? I'd bet not that far. If a salesperson is the most experienced and naturally gifted salesperson on Earth but cannot get motivated to identify and contact prospects, how successful will he or she be? I'd bet not that successful. You get my drift. Motivation is the granddaddy of all skills. You must be motivated and be motivated FIRST if you want any shot at success in any endeavor. There's nothing insignificant or soft about it.

~

Bottom line: In the relationships between a company and its marketplace, a company and its employees, and employees and their company, there are countless ways to create sorethumb opportunities and stick out. Looking for such moments is necessary because it's a whole new ballgame out there.

We live in a business climate where competition is plentiful and fierce. Technology has made it harder to connect and build real relationships. Loyalty is scarce, and buyers are more savvy, sophisticated, and have access to more information than ever before. It's harder than ever to make your mark and stand out. Mediocrity is rampant and excellence is no longer good enough. Customer expectations are sky high.

The only shot a salesperson, or any professional for that matter, has is to be a "sore thumb." And that, I might add, is highly contagious!

A Final Thought or Two...

I recognize that I've covered a lot of ground, so because I am a bottom-line kind of guy, let me leave you with a couple final thoughts that underscore all the things we've explored in this book. I sure hope this book has been helpful from cover to cover, but if you remember only a few things, remember the following.

ALL RELATIONSHIPS ARE PERSONAL AND THUS EMOTIONALLY CHARGED

Everyone understands that personal, romantic relationships are highly emotional and often unpredictable as a result. However, we tend to think of business relationships as being more level-headed and even-keeled. This is simply not true. People are people, and relationships are relationships.

If you get nothing from this book except for the fact that you should look at your business relationships the same way you do your personal ones, you will benefit greatly, and because the relationships are similar, order matters. There is a natural rhythm and order of a relationship that should not be violated if you care about the relationship progressing. You wouldn't ask someone to marry within minutes of meeting him or her—that would be a huge turnoff. It would be premature and grossly out of order. It would bring most prospective relationships to a grinding halt. Yet it seems perfectly acceptable (and even admirable) for salespeople to start closing on their customers immediately after shaking hands for the first time. This has been the conventional school of thought for as long as sales training has been around. The problem is its bad business, and it is not a healthy way to start a relationship. It's out of order.

Selling hasn't changed; the customers have. The twenty-first century is the age of the most sophisticated customer in history. In fact, it will be known as the "age of the consumer." Today's customers don't want people to "sell" them. They want salespeople to help them do their jobs better. They salespeople they can trust. They want salespeople who are on their side and will be partners to their business. They want salespeople who are committed and are loyal. They want real, bona fide relationships. They won't say that because then it becomes forced and less authentic. They play their cards close to the vest, much as they would in a personal relationship when neither person wants to let on their true feelings too soon for fear of getting hurt.

Business may be different in many aspects, but when it comes to people dealing with people, the rules of relationships are immutable. People make decisions based on emotion even though they may explain or justify their decision with logic. Salespeople put far too much emphasis on logical presentations, data, statistics, and case studies, at the expense of genuinely connecting with the customers. Before it's a sale, it's a relationship. People are emotional creatures, and that doesn't change simply because it's business.

PEOPLE DO BUSINESS WITH PEOPLE THEY LIKE

That's pretty simple yet not very easy. As a salesperson, your first and only job is to get the other person to like you. Tricks, techniques, and other insincere tactics will not work. It must be an authentic emotion. You've heard the old saying that the very first sale you make is yourself. This is 100 percent accurate! If your customer likes you and wants to do business with you, the details won't matter. You will find common ground to get a deal done. Logistical differences can be worked out if two people want to work together. However, if your customers don't like you and don't want to work with you, the logistical differences will be insurmountable.

Your job as a professional salesperson couldn't be clearer: it's to build relationships and get your customers to genuinely like you. If you focus on the relationship, the rest will take care of itself. Your success as a salesperson is directly proportional to the quality of your relationships. Getting people to like you is not easy, but it is what separates the average from the great.

This reminds me of a joke about the difficulty of relationships that I like to tell in my seminars. Here goes:

> A woman accompanied her husband to the doctor's office. After her husband's checkup, the doctor called the wife into his office alone. He said, "Your husband is suffering from a very severe disease, combined with horrible stress. If you don't do the following, your husband will surely die."

"Each morning, fix him a healthy breakfast. Be pleasant, and make sure he is in a good mood. For lunch make him a nutritious meal he can take to work. And for dinner, prepare an especially nice meal for him."

"Don't burden him with chores, as this could further his stress. Don't discuss your problems with him; it will only make his stress worse. Try to relax your husband in the evening by giving him plenty of backrubs."

"Encourage him to watch some type of team sporting event on television. And most importantly, make love with your husband several times a week and satisfy his every whim. If you can do this for the next 10 months to a year, I think your husband will regain his health."

On the way home, the husband asked his wife, "What did the doctor say?"

"You're going to die," she replied.

BE CONTAGIOUS!

Whoever said relationships are easy? Relationships can be hard, and business in the twenty-first century can be very unforgiving, but if you're focused on the other person, good things will happen. There is no price that can be put on a great relationship and no substitute for truly connecting, and the secret for that is, BE CONTAGIOUS!

Being contagious is not something you do but rather someone you are. It's a quality, not a skill. Sure, there are a few things you can do that are more contagious than others, and I've written about them throughout this book. But being contagious has and always will come from within. Being contagious is a byproduct of the person you are. All relationships, business and personal, begin with a spark and a connection. There can't be a spark if there's no fire inside. The pilot light must be on. That inner light is the source of contagiousness. It shines through your eyes, is heard in the sound of your voice, is evident by the way you listen, is felt in your handshake, and is seen in the bounce of your step. When you're contagious, people notice it, feel it, like you, and want to do business with you. That's how you sell in today's world. The secret isn't in techniques and tactics. The secret must be in you. The secret is in being contagious, and that has, and always will be, the spark that ignites any relationship.

Index

ABCs of selling, 27, 28, 107
Admit the mistake, 69
Advertising, 191–192
Age of the consumer, 2, 202
AIDA, 54
Ambiguity, 169
Antagonism, 88–89
Apathy, 162, 180
Apple, 184
Art of avoidance, 125
Asking questions, 79–83,
    118–119, 127–129
Assigning blame, 165
Assuming the sale, 109–110
Attention, interest, desire, and
    action (AIDA), 54
Attention span, 33
Authenticity, 11, 68
Author's experiences/beliefs
    bottom-line benefit, 102
    elevator pitch, 94
    first meeting with wife,
        88–89
    first three jobs, 66–67
    sales presentation, 99–100
    seminar ("Ten Tips to a Better
        Price"), 120–121
    6:00 a.m. appointment,
        143–144
    staffing industry expert,
        150–151
    wedding vows, 67
Avoiding failure, 98

Baseball heroes, 23
Be-strategies, 145. See also
    Cultivating the relationship
Be there (regular contact/timely
    follow-up), 156–157

Being sensitive, 58–60
Benefit, 101
Body language, 51
Bottom-line benefit, 102
Brand, 188–189
Breach of trust, 151–155
"Budget," 134–137
Business vs. personal
    relationships, 13, 201–202
Buyers' remorse, 145, 148
Buying signals, 108–109

Captivate and cultivate, 28–29.
    See also Cultivating the
    relationship
Captivation, 142, 158
Caring, 162, 180
Carnegie, Dale, 39
Changing world, 1–2, 8–9
Childlike amazement and
    wonder, 90
Churchill, Winston, 117
Clemente, Roberto, 23
Closed-ended question, 81–82
Closing a sale, 141, 142
Cold selling, 33–52
    enthusiasm/positive attitude,
        35–36
    gatekeeper moment, 41–43
    goals, 38, 40
    handling rejection, 36–37
    initiating contact, 41–43
    interest question. See Interest
        question (IQ)
    map out your day, 38–40
    plan, 41
    preparation, 34–35
Commitment, 68
Commitment to learning, 21

Company policy, 174–177
Company website, 191
Complaints/problems. *See* Crisis management
Concession policy, 154–155
Confidence, 19–20, 68, 110, 141
Consumer age, 2
Consumer choices, 2–3
Contact attempts, 39–41
Contagiousness, 7–8, 12, 18, 206
Continuous learning, 21–22, 192–195
Conviction, 61–63
Corporate education, 120
Corporate relationships. *See* Institutional relationships
Cost, 139, 140
Countersales measure, 76
Coupon, 178–179
Courtship, 14
Crisis management, 159–181
  ambiguity, 169
  assigning blame, 165
  attempt to achieve resolution, 167–170
  calming language, 178
  customer loyalty, and, 162
  dump their bucket (DTB), 166–167
  let customer vent, 166–167
  own the problem, 164–165
  thank the customer, 163–164
  think of complaints as opportunities, 161
  transferring customer to another person, 168–169
  verbalization of complaints, 160–162
  what not to say. *See* What not to say (complaints)
Cultivating curiosity, 74–92
  asking questions, 79–83
  fascination, 90–92

  listening. *See* Listening
  zeroing in, 75–79
Cultivating the relationship, 141–158
  be there (regular contact/timely follow-up), 156–157
  breach of trust, 151–155
  expertise, 149–151
  friendship, 146–149
  go the extra mile, 155–156
  invitations to customer events, 147–148
  keep your word, 152
  loyalty, 151–155
  price integrity, 153–155
  what not to say. *See* What not to say (complaints)
Cultivation, 142
Curiosity, 46, 74. *See also* Cultivating curiosity
Curiosity builder, 191
Customer advocacy, 175
Customer disloyalty, 151
Customer expectations, 2, 6, 200
Customer loyalty, 2, 10, 11
Customer point of view, 44, 48–49, 205
Customer problems and complaints. *See* Crisis management
Customer service, 145, 155
Customer service department, 155–156, 186
Customer service statistics, 161

Daydreaming, 84–85
Debating customers over their decisions, 115–116
Decision making, 110, 118, 137, 203
Dell, Michael, 19
Dictating the next step, 110–112
Disenfranchised customers, 145
Dissatisfied customer, 145

Double-barreled benefit, 49
Dump their bucket (DTB),
    166–167

Education, 192–195
Elevator pitch, 94–95
Emotional decision, 18–20
Employee morale, 192
Endorphins, 197, 198
Energy, 189–192
Enthusiasm/positive
    attitude, 35–36
Error-free ongoing
    relationship, 68
Eureka factor, 17–18
Excellence, 6, 7
Excitement, 35–36
Excuses, 12–13
Expect to sell, 109–110, 141
Expertise, 149–151
Eye contact, 51, 62, 106
Eyes, 61–63, 89–90, 122–123

Facebook, 5
Fact finding, 82–83
False courtesy, 89
Fascination, 90–92
Fast rate/high inflection (FRHI)
    speakers, 57–58
Fast rate/low inflection (FRLI)
    speakers, 57
Faxes, 5
Fear of loss, 98
Feature, 101
First impressions, 16–17, 33,
    52, 53
Flinch, 133–134
Focus on the customer, 205
Formal presentation. *See* Sales
    presentation
Friendship, 146–149

Gain an advantage/avoid a
    disadvantage, 97–98

Gatekeeper moment, 41–43
Gibson, Kirk, 23
Giving too much information,
    101
Go the extra mile, 155–156
Golden rule, 59, 154
Google, 184
Great service and selling skills,
    6–7

Handling rejection, 36–37,
    116–117
Handshake, 51–52
Hard skill, 198
Honesty, 68, 69
Hope to gain, 98
Humility, 68–71

"I don't know," 69–70
In Search of Excellence (Peters), 6
Indifference, 180
Individual formula, 39–40
Inflection, 55–60. *See also* Vocal
    patterns
Information gathering, 82–83
Information overload, 108
Initial prospecting stage. *See*
    Cold selling
Institutional purchasing, 120
Institutional relationships,
    183–200
  advertising, 191–192
  brand, 188–189
  company-employee
    relationships, 192–199
  company-marketplace
    relationships, 185–192
  company website, 191
  educating the employees,
    192–195
  energy, 189–192
  motivation, 195–199
  reputation, 185–188
  telephone greeting, 190–191

Integrity, 68
Interest question (IQ), 43–52
  connection, 45–46
  example, 49–50
  greeting, 44
  icing, 49
  multiple IQs, 51
  problem, 46–48
  reason, 45
  sound natural/look confident,
    50–52
Internet presence, 191
Invitations to customer events,
    147–148

Jobs, Steve, 19
John, Elton, 189
Jumping to conclusions, 88

Keep your word, 152
Kissing, 28
Knight, Philip, 19
Knowledge, 150

Law of excitement, 35
Learning, 21–22, 192–195
Learning libraries, 193–194
Lee Resource study, 160
Likeability, 203
Lincoln, Abe, 194
Listening, 83–90, 128
  act of caring, 89
  antagonism, 88–89
  daydreaming, 84–85
  evaluating the dialogue,
    85–86
  eyes, 89–90
  false courtesy, 89
  jumping to conclusions, 88
  physical distraction, 85
  rule of thumb, 92
  sales presentation, 93
  selectiveness, 87
  silent debate, 86–87

  speeding things up, 86
  strategizing, 86
Love at first sight, 61
Love what you do, 22–24
Loyalty, 151–155

Magnetic pull, 16
Magnetic push, 17
Making decisions, 110,
    118, 137, 203
Matching a competitor's price,
    178–179
MBIs, 123–125
Memorized
    presentation, 99
Mental preparation, 35
Mirroring, 58
Motivation, 195–199
Motivators, 98
Multiple buying influences
    (MBIs), 123–125

Natural rhythm/order, 25–27,
    79, 95, 202
Needs analysis, 91
Negative banter, 197
Neutral territory, 126
New *vs.* existing
    customers, 177
"NEXT!", 37
Note taking, 82

Objections, 119
One-sided prospecting, 48
Ongoing learning, 192–195
Open-ended question, 80–81
Opening statement, 77–78
Optimism, 197
Order/natural rhythm, 25–27,
    79, 95, 202
Order of a successful
    sales call, 95
Order taking, 114
Outline, 99–100

Overselling, 108–109
Overuse of technology, 105–106

Paralinguistics, 54. *See also* Vocal
 patterns
Passion, 22–24
Peers, 46, 47
Personal apology, 165
Personal development library, 22
Personal questions, 127
Peters, Tom, 6
Pitch, 94–95
Play off the competition,
 138–140
Poker analogy, 6
Positive attitude, 35–36
Presence, 20, 60–71
 conviction, 61–63
 defined, 60
 humility, 68–71
 purpose, 64–68
Presentation. *See* Sales
 presentation
Price integrity, 153–155
Price/pricing, 113–140
 asking questions, 118–119,
  127–129
 "budget," 134–137
 downplay your needs, 129–130
 eyes, 122–123
 face-to-face meetings, 125–127
 flinch, 133–134
 matching a competitor's price,
  178–179
 maybe response, 117–120
 multiple buying influences
  (MBIs), 123–125
 no response, 115–117
 play off the competition,
  138–140
 price integrity, 153–155
 price is too high, 12–13
 price *vs.* cost comparison,
  139–140

sales based on price, 122
 sales presentation, 111, 114
 stalling, 137–138
 take charge, 127–129
 upfront price question, 26–27,
  96, 130–133
 yes response, 115
Price *vs.* cost comparison,
 139–140
Pride in the job, 65, 66
Proactive post-closing strategies.
 See Cultivating the
 relationship
Problem prospects, 133
Professional athletes, 23
Psychologically ready to sell,
 35, 41
Psychosomatic
 conditions, 197
Purpose, 64–68

Question asking, 79–83,
 118–119, 127–129

Reading, 21, 22, 194
Reason, 64
Rejection, 36–37, 116–117
Relationship of convenience, 11
Relationships, 13, 14, 31
 admit the mistake, 69
 business *vs.* personal, 13,
  201–202
 customer's point of view, 44,
  48–49
 errors/mistakes, 68. *See also*
  Crisis management
 feelings/emotions, 17–25,
  201–203
 friendship, 146–149
 golden rule, 59
 institutional. *See* Institutional
  relationships
 invite inclusion, 70–71
 likeability, 203

Relationships (*contd.*)
  loyalty, 151–155
  mutual value and trust,
    121–122
  natural rhythm and order,
    25–27, 79, 95, 202
  ongoing process, 29–31, 157.
    See also Cultivating the
    relationship
  stay in touch, 156–157
  success, and, 204
  two-way street, 71, 174
Reputation, 185–188
Rhythm altering questions, 26
Rich, David. *See* Author's
    experiences/beliefs
Ripken, Cal, 23
Rocky start, 89
Romancenomics
  closing, 27–29
  defined, 13–14
  feelings, 17–25
  first impressions, 16–17
  ongoing relationship, 29–30
  timing/order, 25–27
Rose, Pete, 23

Sales crusade, 64
Sales presentation, 93–112
  assuming the sale, 109–110
  customer feedback, 107
  dictating the next step,
    110–112
  duration, 109
  elevator pitch, 94–95
  eye contact, 106
  features/benefits, 101–102
  from general to specific,
    100–101
  organization, 98–100
  outline, 99–100
  overselling, 108–109
  overuse of technology,
    105–106
  possible customer
    responses, 114
  series of smaller yeses, 107
  "stories," 100
  timing/order, 95
  transition statement, 96–97
  uniqueness, 102–104
  voice pattern, 104–105
Sales technique, 10
Savvy buyers, 10
Seals & Crofts, 153
Seinfeld, 128
Selective listening, 87
Self-assuredness, 68
Selling, 157, 202
Selling basics, 8
Series of smaller yeses, 107
Shallow act of show-and-tell,
    75–76
Shifting the goal, 30
Shortcuts, 96
Shotgun approach, 101, 108
Silent debate, 86–87
Sincerity/genuineness/inner
    light, 206
Skill, 198
Slow rate/high inflection (SRHI)
    speakers, 55–56
Slow rate/low inflection (SRLI)
    speakers, 56
Small steps, 38–40
Snipe approach, 101
Soft skill, 198
Somapsychotic conditions, 197
"Someone Saved My Life
    Tonight" (John), 189
Sore-thumb principle, 184.
    See also Institutional
    relationships
Sparks of interest, 33
Speaking patterns. *See*
    Vocal patterns
Speed of information retrieval, 5
Stalling, 137–138

Stay in the moment, 157
Stay in touch, 156–157
Strategizing, 86
Style flexing, 58

Taking charge
    opening statement, 78
    price, 127–129
    relinquishing role of
        expert, 129
    sales presentation, 111–112
Taking notes, 82
Talking too much, 92, 115
Technology, 3–5, 39, 200
Telephone, put customer on
    hold, 173
Telephone greeting, 190–191
Thank-you notes, 156
Timing/order, 25–27, 79, 95, 202
Touch points, 189–190
Transition statement, 96–97
Truman, Harry, 21
Trust, 151–152
Turnover, 9

Uniqueness, 102–104
United Airlines commercial, 4
Upfront price question, 26–27,
    96, 130–133
Uplifting language, 197

Vendor, 146–147, 149
Venting, 166–167
Verbal game of tennis, 119
Vision, 20
Vocal patterns, 54–60
    fast rate/high inflection
        (FRHI) speakers, 57–58

fast rate/low inflection (FRLI)
    speakers, 57
match customer's speech
    pattern, 58–60
sales presentation, 104–105
slow rate/high inflection
    (SRHI) speakers, 55–56
slow rate/low inflection (SRLI)
    speakers, 56
Vulnerability, 68

"What do you think?", 70–71
What not to say (complaints),
    171–179
    ASAP, 172
    "call back later," 174
    company policy, 174–177
    coupon, 178–179
    "it wasn't my
        fault," 172–173
    put customer on hold, 173
    "stop bugging me," 180
    "that's not my
        department," 180
    "what was your name,"
        171–172
    "what's the problem,"
        177–178
"What that means
    to you," 102
Word of mouth, 2, 3
Words, 171
Wow-able, 6

"You may be right," 70

Zeroing in, 75–79
Ziglar, Zig, 21, 35

About the Author

David Rich is founder and president of Rich Ideas, a speaking and corporate education company dedicated to inspiring people to be "contagious." He has been speaking to association and corporate audiences for over 25 years.

He has been called, "The Most Personable Speaker in America!" and is one of the nation's leading experts on persuasion, motivation and creating personal and organizational "contagiousness." Since 1986, he has presented to over one million people in 46 states and 4 countries. David is one of less than 500 speakers in the world to be designated a Certified Speaking Professional, the highest earned designation in the speaking profession.

David has presented to groups ranging in size from small local churches to the Fortune 100 companies. His corporate clients include AT&T, Goodyear, Coca-Cola, Sears, Gillette, Kellogg's, PBS, and the U.S. Chamber of Commerce. His association clients include, Society of Consumer Affairs Professionals, National Association of Manufacturers, National Association of Catering Executives, American Staffing Association, and the International Customer Service Association.

His writings have appeared in numerous national and trade magazines, including Personal Selling Power and Inc. magazine. He has also written the following books: *How to Stay Motivated on a Daily Basis!* (Kendall-Hunt, 1995) and *How to Click with Everyone Every Time!* (McGraw-Hill, 2004). In 2006, David released 7 *Biblical Truths You Won't Hear in Church, But Might Change Your Life!* (Harvest House, 2006), and in 2008, *You Mean That Isn't in the Bible?: 10 Popular Beliefs That Simply Aren't True!* (Harvest House, 2008)

David can be reached through his websites: www.contagioustalk.com or www.Gracecamp.com.